SERIES TITLES

PREHISTORY **I**   **XIII** SETTLING THE AMERICAS

MESOPOTAMIA AND THE BIBLE LANDS **II**   **XIV** ASIAN AND AFRICAN EMPIRES

ANCIENT EGYPT AND GREECE **III**   **XV** THE INDUSTRIAL REVOLUTION

THE ROMAN WORLD **IV**   **XVI** ENLIGHTENMENT AND REVOLUTION

ASIAN CIVILIZATIONS **V**   **XVII** NATIONALISM AND THE ROMANTIC MOVEMENT

AMERICAS AND THE PACIFIC **VI**   **XVIII** THE AGE OF EMPIRE

EARLY MEDIEVAL TIMES **VII**   **XIX** NORTH AMERICA: EXPANSION, CIVIL WAR, AND EMERGENCE

BEYOND EUROPE **VIII**   **XX** TURN OF THE CENTURY AND THE GREAT WAR

LATE MEDIEVAL EUROPE **IX**   **XXI** VERSAILLES TO WORLD WAR II

RENAISSANCE EUROPE **X**   **XXII** 1945 TO THE COLD WAR

VOYAGES OF DISCOVERY **XI**   **XXIII** 1991 TO THE 21ST CENTURY

BIRTH OF MODERN NATIONS **XII**   **XXIV** ISSUES TODAY

BEYOND EUROPE
was created and produced by McRae Books Srl
Via del Salviatino, 1 — 50016 — Fiesole
(Florence), (Italy)
info@mcraebooks.com
www.mcraebooks.com

Publishers: Anne McRae, Marco Nardi
Series Editor: Anne McRae
Author: John Malam and Neil Morris
Main Illustrations: Giorgio Bacchin pp. 20–21;
Francesca D'Ottavi pp. 24–25; Emmanuelle Etienne
pp. 12–13; G. Gaudenzi p. 22b; Sabrina Marconi pp.
8–9; MM comunicazione (M. Cappon, M. Favilli,G.
Sbragi, C. Scutti) pp. 11, 14–15, 30–31, 42–43t;
Tiziano Perotto pp. 44–45; Claudia Saraceni pp.
18–19, 29t; Sergio pp. 40–41b

Other illustrations: Studio Stalio (Alessandro Cantucci,
Fabiano Fabbrucci)
Maps: M. Paola Baldanzi
Photos: © Dean Conger/Corbis p. 7; © Lowell
Georgia/Corbis p. 17t; ©Copyright the Trustees of The
British Museum pp. 32–33; © Lonely Planet Images /
Glenn Beanland p.35t; Marco Nardi p. 37b; © Paul C.
Pet/zefa/Corbis p. 38b
Art Director: Marco Nardi
Layouts: Starry Dogs Books Ltd.
Project Editor: Loredana Agosta
Research: Lucy Turner Voakes, Loredana Agosta
Editing: Tall Tree Ltd, London
Repro: Litocolor, Florence

Consultants:

Dr. Gregory Possehl is an anthropological
archaeologist with broad interests in the development
of urbanisation in the Old World. His specific research
and writing have focused on the first phase of
urbanisation in South Asia, namely in the ancient
cities of Mohenjo-Daro and Harappa. He has been
conducting field research and excavations in India
since 1979.

Library of Congress Cataloging-in-Publication Data

Morris, Neil, 1946-
  Beyond Europe / Neil Morris and John Malam.
    p. cm. -- (History of the world ; 8)
  Includes index.
  Summary: "A detailed overview of the history of
non-European parts of the world from 500 to 1500,
including Africa, China, Japan, Korea, Southeast Asia,
and India"--Provided by publisher.
  ISBN 978-8860981516
  1. Middle Ages--Juvenile literature. 2. Civilization,
Medieval--Juvenile literature. I. Malam, John, 1957-
II. Title.
  D117.M68 2009
  909'.1--dc22

                                        2008008406

Printed and bound in Malaysia.

Beyond Europe

Neil Morris and John Malam

Consultants: Dr. Gregory Possehl, Professor of Archeology, Department of Anthropology, University of Pennsylvania and Curator of the Asian Section, University of Pennsylvania Museum of Archaeology and Anthropology.

Zak
BOOKS

Contents

5 Introduction

6 Africa and Asia

8 The First African States

10 Early African Kingdoms

12 Trading Empires

14 Christianity and Islam

16 The Tang Dynasty

18 The Song Dynasty

20 Chinese Influence in Asia

22 The Mongol Invasion

24 Mongol Rule

26 Asuka and Nara Japan

28 Heian Period in Japan

30 Japan Under the Shoguns

32 The Kingdoms of Korea

34 Southeast Asian Kingdoms

36 Southeast Asian Culture

38 Northern India and the Deccan

40 The Chola Empire

42 Southern India and Sri Lanka

44 Muslim Rule in India

46 Glossary

47 Index

The Chinese love of nature is clear from this silk tapestry of a landscape, made in about 1100.

Note—This book shows dates as related to the conventional beginning of our era, or the year 1, understood as the year of the birth of Jesus Christ. All events dating before this year are listed as BCE (Before Current Era). Events dating after that year are defined as CE (Current Era).

TIMELINE

	500 BCE	500 CE	625	750
AFRICA	Ironworking begins in the Nok culture. First permanent settlements in Jenne-jeno.		The Christian kingdom of Axum in decline. Emergence of the kingdom of Ghana.	Founding of the kingdom of Kanem near Lake Chad.
CHINA			The Tang Dynasty is established.	Period of good government and flourishing of the arts.
JAPAN		Buddhism introduced to Japan from Korea. Asuka period begins. Chinese-style government comes to Japan.	Heijokyo (Nara) becomes first permanent capital.	Heian period begins when the capital is moved to Heiankyo (Kyoto).
KOREA			The kingdom of Silla defeats the kingdom of Paekche. Munmu Wang becomes the first ruler of unified Korea.	
SOUTHEAST ASIA	Cham kingdom period begins in Vietnam.		Rebellion in Vietnam crushed by China.	Khmer kingdom period in Cambodia begins.
INDIA			Harsha Empire period begins.	Buddhism flourishes in eastern India. Reign of the first Chola king.

Introduction

Although separated by thousands of miles, the ancient cultures of Africa, India, China, Japan, and Southeast Asia had much in common. During the Medieval period in these regions states emerged with powerful warrior kings at their head. When kingdoms defeated their rivals in battle, empires were sometimes born. Some lasted for centuries, but others flourished briefly and then died. In the thousand years after 500 CE, these regions developed the cultural identities we recognize today. Styles of art and architecture came to characterize each culture. Religion knew no boundaries and crossed borders to take root among new adherents, while merchants plied their trade across the sea and along land routes in search of exotic goods.

Only the most important people in the city-state of Benin, west Africa, had valuable bronze objects such as this water vessel in the shape of a leopard.

At Angkor, capital of the Khmer Empire in Cambodia, stone faces stare out from the side of a stone tower, as they have done for more than a thousand years.

875	1000	1125	1250	1375
	Formation of the Yoruba state of Ife.	Foundation of the kingdom of Benin.	Mali becomes the most powerful West African state. Stone houses are built in Zimbabwe.	
Five dynasties rule a divided empire. Beginning of the Song Dynasty.		The Song capital of Kaifeng falls to Jin invaders from Manchuria.	Reign of Khubilai Khan, first ruler of the Yuan Dynasty. The northern Jin Empire is conquered by the Mongols.	
		Kamakura period begins.	Japanese armies defeat Mongol invasions from China.	
		Japan's first shogun is appointed; a new form of government begins.	Kamakura period ends after rebellion; a new family rises to power.	
The Koryo Kingdom begins.			Period of Mongol invasions from China.	Koryo Kingdom ends.
			Peace treaty signed with the Mongol invaders.	
			Start of Mongol incursions into Southeast Asia.	
		Khmer capital at Angkor briefly captured by the Chams.	Chiang Mai kingdom period in Thailand begins.	
Hindu temples are built at Chandella kingdom capital. Cholas conquer rival Pallavas and Pandyas.	Parts of northern India controlled by Muslim states. Cholas raid Southeast Asia.	Delhi becomes capital of the Sultanate of Delhi, an Islamic kingdom.	The end of the Chola Empire.	Hindu kingdom of Vijayanagar in southern India defeats Muslim forces.

EARLY AFRICA AND ASIA

224–651
Rule of the Sassanid Dynasty in Persia.

300–710
The Kofun period in Japan.

395
The Roman Empire is split in two (the Western Empire run from Rome, the Eastern Empire from Constantinople).

442
Roman provinces in North Africa are conquered by invading Vandals.

c. 570–632
Life of the Prophet Muhammad.

618
The Tang dynasty seizes power from the Sui Dynasty in China.

651
End of the rule of the Sassanid Dynasty and the Sassanian Empire in Persia.

661–750
The Umayyad Dynasty rules the Islamic world from Damascus.

1453
The Byzantine Empire falls to the Ottoman Turks.

This 9th-century dish from Iraq is inscribed in Kufic script (from the town of Kufah).

Africa and Asia

In Medieval times improvements in farming and technology led to a rise in population and the growth of cities along rivers in Africa and Asia. Jenne-jeno (in present-day Mali) became an important trading city on the River Niger. At the same time, China was an advanced civilisation, where the city of Chang'an grew beside the River Huang He, at the eastern end of the Silk Road.

Roman North Africa

From the 2nd century BCE, the northern coastal region of Africa was colonised by the Romans and became part of their great Empire. The region, which provided huge quantities of wheat and olive oil, became known as the "granary of Rome". In the 5th century CE, while Rome itself was being attacked by Visigoths, Germanic Vandals crossed from the Iberian peninsula and conquered the Roman provinces in North Africa.

Terracotta figure from the ancient Nok culture of West Africa.

Spreading South

Ancient Africa was never a single culture, as the continent's regions developed at different times. The north had a great heritage from the Egyptian civilisation and from the Roman Empire. To the west, ironworking began with the Nok people (see page 8), and technology spread south with the migration of Bantu-speaking people. Great trading empires developed in western Africa.

Asian Dynasties

In Medieval times, Asian civilisations were ruled by a succession of powerful dynasties. In China, the Sui emperors were succeeded by the Tang and then the Song. The Chinese greatly influenced Japan and Korea. In India, the great Gupta Dynasty was brought to an end by invasions from central Asia.

This 1st-century CE Roman plate portrays Africa as a woman.

This tomb guardian dates from the Tang period in China (618–907).

EMPIRES IN 500 CE

EUROPE
ROME •
CONSTANTINOPLE
DAMASCUS •
• CTESIPHON
River Tigris
NUBIA
• JENNE-JENO
River Niger
• AXUM
AFRICA
EMPIRE OF THE RUANRUAN
EMPIRE OF THE HEPHTHALITES
River Huang He
CHANG-AN •
GUPTA EMPIRE
KOREA
JAPAN
INDIAN OCEAN

Conflicting Empires

Two empires ruled in western Asia before the rise of Islam. Sassanid kings ruled Persia from their capital on the River Tigris. They were Zoroastrians and were frequently at war with Christian Byzantines, who ran their empire from Constantinople, capital of the Eastern Roman (or Byzantine) Empire. Muslim Arabs ended the Sassanian Empire in the 7th century, while the Byzantine Empire lasted another 800 years.

- Qi empire
- Eastern Roman Empire
- African kingdoms
- Asian empires
- Sassanian Empire

Religions

In the centuries leading up to the advent of Islam in the 7th century, established religions continued to spread across Asia and Africa. Buddhism spread from India to China along the Silk Road, and from there to Korea and Japan. Another form of Buddhism followed a southern sea route to Southeast Asia. Muslims began spreading into Africa in 640, just eight years after the death of Muhammad.

This Buddha statue in the Yungang caves of China dates from about 460.

Mural of a cross from Nubia (southern Egypt and Sudan). The Coptic Christian church survived in Egypt, though many Copts converted to Islam in the 7th century.

EARLY AFRICA

c. 500 BCE
Ironworking begins in the Nok culture, which flourishes for the next 700 years.

300 BCE
First permanent settlements in Jenne-jeno.

c. 200 BCE
Emergence of Berber kingdoms in northern Africa.

200 BCE–100 CE
The Saharan region becomes drier, pushing people south.

146 BCE
The Romans destroy the city of Carthage, on the North African coast.

1–100 CE
The kingdom of Axum emerges.

350 CE
Axum captures the neighboring Kushite city of Meroë. Axumite king Ezana converts to Christianity.

400 CE
City walls are built at Jenne-jeno.

c. 540 CE
The people of Nubia (in present-day Sudan) are converted to Christianity.

The First African States

About 4,000 years ago, people from the regions of present-day Nigeria and Cameroon started to spread south and east. This may have been caused by the drying of the Sahara. As people formed new settlements, they traded with others. Trade helped to spread metalworking, and the new Iron Age brought about the first African states. By about 500 BCE, people of the Nok culture were using iron. A thousand years later, ironworking and cattle-rearing had spread to southern Africa.

This adze was used for shaving wood. A bolt secures its iron blade to the wooden handle.

The Iron Age

Ironworkers built furnaces of clay and filled them with charcoal. They then used bellows to raise the temperature of the burning fuel. The new technology of ironworking spread southward from the Nok region, and by 300 BCE it had reached the Congo River. Iron was used for making tools and weapons such as knives, spears, and hoes. It soon became a valuable trade item.

Nok Culture

The Nok culture emerged in the hills and lowlands of the region where the Niger and Benue rivers meet in present-day Nigeria. Its people were farmers, who also hunted and gathered food. They lived in mud huts and produced lifelike terra-cotta figures of people and animals. The Nok people learned to smelt iron and took their skills and technology to other regions south of the Sahara Desert.

Above: Nok terracotta head of a bearded man. His shaven head has a single ridge of hair.

The Nok people smelted iron in round furnaces with clay walls. Burning charcoal was heated to high temperatures by blowing air in through holes at the base of the furnace.

The City of Jenne-jeno

Jenne-jeno grew up in the delta region of the River Niger, in present-day Mali. It was built on a central mound, to keep out the river's annual floods. The people lived by herding, fishing and growing crops. Later, Jenne-jeno developed into a thriving trading city and its metalworkers used iron to make tools and jewelry.

This terra-cotta sculpture from Jenne-jeno shows a couple wearing metal jewelry around their necks, wrists, and ankles.

Early African States

This map shows the location of the first kingdoms of Africa. It also indicates the spread of Bantu-speaking peoples southward and eastward from West Africa. The Bantu languages were spread by the migration of farmers who had learned to work iron. This migration occurred gradually, as small groups of people separated from others and moved to new regions. Bantu culture also included the Khoisan-speaking herders and hunter-gatherers of eastern and southern Africa.

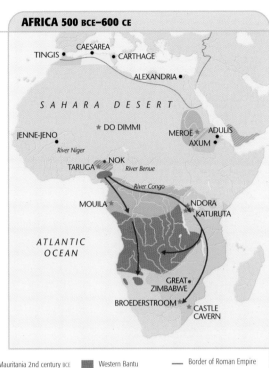

AFRICA 500 BCE–600 CE

TINGIS • CAESAREA • CARTHAGE
ALEXANDRIA •
SAHARA DESERT
DO DIMMI
JENNE-JENO
MEROË ★ ADULIS
AXUM
River Niger
TARUGA ★ NOK
River Benue
River Congo
MOUILA ★
NDORA
KATURUTA
ATLANTIC OCEAN
GREAT ZIMBABWE
BROEDERSTROOM ★ CASTLE CAVERN

Axum c. 350 CE	Mauritania 2nd century BCE	Western Bantu
Occupied by Axum 522–574	Meroë 590 BCE–350 CE	Numidia 2nd century BCE
Eastern Bantu	Nok culture 500 BCE–500 CE	Bantu-speaking people
Northwestern Bantu		

— Border of Roman Empire
➡ Spread of Bantu
★ Iron-producing site

This tall granite monolith is still standing at Axum. Such structures may have represented multi-storey buildings and were probably put up to honor rulers of the kingdom.

This bronze coin from Axum shows a Christian cross.

The Rise of Axum

The kingdom of Axum stretched across the high plains region of present-day northern Ethiopia. It centered on the city of Axum, where there were monumental buildings and stone monoliths. The kingdom became an important trading center, and valuable goods such as ivory, obsidian, and incense passed through the Red Sea port of Adulis.

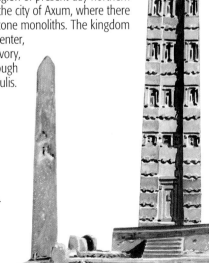

This sculpture was carved from a block of sandstone in the kingdom of Meroë (in present-day Sudan). Two lions flank a ram, and all three animals represent deities. The sculpture was originally set in the walls of a temple.

Early African Kingdoms

After 650 CE, several African kingdoms emerged as population grew in different parts of the continent. Many of the smaller chiefdoms to the south of the Sahara Desert were linked by regional trade routes, and some joined together to form kingdoms. Trade in precious metals and other goods created wealth, and powerful kings lived luxuriously in splendid palaces. By the 13th century, the first city-states were appearing in southern Africa.

This terra-cotta figure from Mali dates from about the 14th century.

Yoruba and Ife

Yoruba-speaking peoples set up several city-states in the forest region of present-day Nigeria. The most powerful Yoruba kingdoms were Ife and Oyo, and Ife eventually emerged as the cultural center of the region. The Yoruba had their own complex religion, based on the worship of hundreds of gods. They produced brilliant sculptures of terra-cotta and bronze.

This bronze sculpture was made in the 12th century by Yoruba craftworkers from Ife.

Mali and Songhai

The powerful Mali empire stretched all the way from the Atlantic coast to Gao and Timbuktu in the east. The empire covered much of modern Gambia, Guinea, Mali, and Senegal. Its wealth and power were based on its trading cities, where gold and ivory were exchanged for goods such as salt and cloth. In the 15th century, Mali was taken over by the Songhai empire.

EARLY AFRICAN KINGDOMS

c. 600 CE
The Christian kingdom of Axum declines, and its capital is later abandoned.

c. 650
Emergence of the kingdom of Ghana.

c. 750
Founding of the kingdom of Kanem near Lake Chad.

975
Axum is destroyed by invaders from the southeast.

c. 1000
Formation of the Yoruba state of Ife (in present-day Nigeria).

c. 1150
Foundation of the kingdom of Benin (in present-day Nigeria).

1250
Mali becomes the most powerful West African state. The stone-walled city of Great Zimbabwe is at the centre of a Shona state.

1312–1337
Reign of Mali ruler Mansa Musa, who expanded his kingdom and spread Islam.

c. 1464
The Songhai Empire conquers Mali.

Kings and Kingdoms

African rulers had great power, and many were extremely wealthy. There may have been a ranking order among the rulers of city-states. In the Yoruba states, for example, the king of Ife outranked the others. In Benin, the king controlled all foreign trade and commissioned skilled metalworkers to create royal busts and plaques.

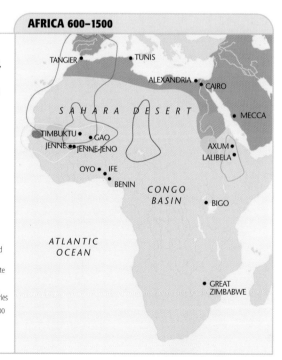

AFRICA 600–1500

TANGIER • • TUNIS
ALEXANDRIA • • CAIRO
S A H A R A   D E S E R T
• MECCA
TIMBUKTU • • GAO
JENNE • • JENNE-JENO
AXUM •
LALIBELA •
OYO • • IFE
• BENIN
C O N G O   B A S I N
• BIGO
ATLANTIC OCEAN
• GREAT ZIMBABWE

Alwa c. 350–1505	Ethiopia, founded c. 1100
Ghana c. 350–1505	Almoravid emirate 1056–1147
Makkura c. 600–1317	Kanem-Bornu c. 11th–19th centuries
Takrur c. 800–1100	Mali c. 1200–1500
Axum c. 1 CE–975	Songhai c. 1240–1590

This brass head of a queen from Benin was probably made to be placed at an altar for the veneration of female ancestors. Benin queens shared with kings and chief warriors the privilege of being able to wear a crown.

This bronze plaque from Benin shows a ruler with his attendants.

Benin

From the 12th century, clans of the Bini (or Edo) people of Benin were led by local chieftains. Later they paid tribute to an overall ruler, known as the "oba." During the 15th century, the people of Benin formed trade links with the Portuguese sailors who had arrived in Africa. Benin metalworkers became well known for their skill in casting brass and bronze, while other craftsmen carved ivory.

Kingdom of Ghana

The first great empire in West Africa was Wagadu, also known as Ghana, which lay between the Senegal and Niger rivers (in parts of present-day Mauritania and Mali). This kingdom grew rich by trading gold, which was exchanged for copper and valuable slabs of salt from Saharan mines. Ghana flourished between the 8th and the 11th centuries. The king of Ghana charged a tax in gold on all goods that traveled into and out of his kingdom.

The king of Ghana is surrounded by his court as he receives his people. The ruler claimed all gold that was found in his kingdom.

Great Zimbabwe

In southern Africa, stone-walled enclosures were built from the 10th century. These small cities formed a trading network that was linked to the east coast. The largest of the cities was Great Zimbabwe, meaning "great stone houses." This was at the center of the Shona Empire that flourished from the 12th to the 15th century.

Here, the stone wall of Great Zimbabwe surrounds the houses of the elite.

An 11th-century gold coin from the island of Pemba, to the north of Kilwa.

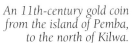

This gold-plated rhino, found in southern Africa, dates from about the 12th century.

Trading Empires

African kingdoms grew wealthy through trade, which increased when Muslim merchants traveled south from the Mediterranean region. In East Africa, Swahili-speaking Islamic settlements grew into important city-states. The most valued trading item was gold, much of which was mined in the forests of the Akan region to the south of the Mali Empire. Gold increasingly became a common currency for merchants, as the trading network spread out across the continent.

Coastal City-States

From about 1200 CE, Swahili city-states on the coast of East Africa grew into thriving commercial centers. They stretched down the coast from Mogadishu (in modern Somalia) to Malindi (in present-day Kenya) and Kilwa (in Tanzania). Goods from the African interior passed through their ports, which developed a thriving sea trade. From the coast on the Indian Ocean gold and ivory were exported to Arabia and India. Some of the states, including Kilwa, became independent Muslim sultanates.

Caravans took many weeks to travel across the Sahara.

MAJOR TRADING ROUTES

TANGIER
MEDITERRANEAN SEA
CAIRO
ARABIA
TAOUDENNI
TIMBUKTU
AXUM
KUMBI SALEH
AKAN REGION
MOGADISHU
MALINDI
PEMBA ISLAND
INDIAN OCEAN
KILWA
ATLANTIC OCEAN
GREAT ZIMBABWE

Distribution of Zimbabwe-style sites • City by the 15th century → Trade routes to Asia — Trans-Saharan trade route

Routes
The Mediterranean coastal region was linked to the kingdoms of West Africa by established trade routes across the desert. Traders traveled in caravans of many camels, stopping at mining settlements on the way. Further south, many routes led to the east coast. There, the developing sea trade of the ports and coastal states on the Indian Ocean linked Africa with Arabia, India, and China.

Goods
As well as the salt and copper that were mined in the Sahara, many other goods were transported across the desert. Pottery, glass, and other luxury items were brought from the north. They were exchanged for gold, ivory, and ebony from the forests and grasslands of the south. The East African city-states traded gold, ivory, and slaves from the African interior. They also dealt in other metals, such as copper and iron, as well as precious emeralds, spices, and animal skins. In exchange they received cotton, silk, and porcelain from Asia.

Swahili traders sailed from the coast of East Africa in merchant boats such as this mtepe.

Elephant tusks such as this were prized for their ivory, which was an important trading item.

Across the Sahara
Camels were introduced into Saharan Africa in about 100 BCE, and they were used to transport heavy goods across the desert. Salt and copper were mined in the desert itself. Slabs of solid salt were dug out of open mines at places such as Taoudenni (in modern Mali) and transported south to Kumbi Saleh and Timbuktu, which grew into wealthy trading cities.

AFRICAN TRADERS

c. 100
In a work entitled The Periplus of the Erytharaean, *an anonymous Greek traveler describes the busy Arab trade along the coasts of East Africa.*

c. 250
Kingdom of Axum controls trade on the Red Sea.

c. 750
Rise in Trans-saharan trade activity.

c. 800
Towns on the East-African coast become established trading centers.

c. 1250
Stone houses are built in Zimbabwe.

Christianity and Islam

A 14th-century illuminated gadl, *an account of the lives of the saints, from Ethiopia.*

According to tradition, the first Christian community in Africa was formed in Alexandria, Egypt, by the apostle Mark in 60 CE. From there, Christianity spread both west and east, until Muslims from Arabia arrived with their new religion of Islam in the 7th century. The Muslims quickly conquered the Mediterranean coastal strip, and as the Islamic empire expanded, the Christians were left with individual regions such as Ethiopia.

A 14th-century processional cross from Lalibela, Ethiopia. Some holy days such as the Epiphany were celebrated with magnificent processions.

RELIGION IN AFRICA

c. 570–632
Life of the Prophet Muhammad in Arabia.

642
Muslims invade Egypt.

661–750
Rule of the Muslim Umayyad Dynasty, including North Africa, from Damascus.

750–1258
Rule of Muslim Abbasid caliphs from Baghdad.

1098
Saharan Berber Almoravid leader Yusuf adopts the title "Ruler of the Muslims."

1130
Berber Almohads attack the Almoravid capital of Marrakech.

1240–1255
Sundiata Keita rules the Mali Empire, and converts to Islam.

c. 1475
Timbuktu and Djenné become centers of Muslim learning.

Religious Art

Islamic artists, who were required not to show images of living things, developed their own distinctive style of geometric designs. By contrast, the Christian art of Ethiopia was full of human figures and scenes from the gospels, many shown as wooden and metal icons. In Egypt, Coptic art was influenced by Roman and Byzantine traditions, and many Coptic artists concentrated on designing textiles.

The Spread of Christianity

By 500 CE, Christianity was widespread in northeast Africa. Egypt was controlled from Byzantium, the capital of the East Roman empire, and many Egyptians belonged to a Christian church known as Coptic (from the Arabic word for "Egyptian"). Further south, the kingdom of Axum had been Christian since 350 CE. The people of Nubia (part of modern Sudan) converted to Christianity during the 6th century.

Islamic Invaders

Muslims entered Africa from the Arabian Peninsula. They converted Berber tribes on their way across North Africa, and some Berbers joined the Muslim force that crossed to the Iberian peninsula in 711. Muslim invaders traveled across the Sahara Desert, while traders and settlers made their way down the coast of East Africa. By 1500, Islam had spread over much of northern Africa, reaching down the eastern coast. The states of Alwa, Ethiopia, and the Congo remained Christian.

A Muslim Arab cavalryman. Muslim soldiers were effective conquerors, with a strong belief that they were doing God's will.

The mud-brick mosque at Djenné grew up beside ancient Jenne-jeno. By the 15th century, Djenné was a center of Muslim learning.

Page from a 14th-century Qu'ran from Northern Africa.

Mosques and Churches

As well as being places for communal prayer, mosques were centers of Muslim social life and learning. Great mosques were built during the 12th century, including the Kutubiya Mosque in Marrakech and the Kizimkazi Mosque in Zanzibar, which dates from 1107. Christians also built churches in East Africa. The most famous were rock-hewn structures built by a king named Lalibela of the Zagwe Dynasty, which ruled Ethiopia from 1173 to 1270.

One of the 11 churches that were carved out of the granite hills at Roha, now named Lalibela, in Ethiopia.

The Tang Dynasty

In China, the period of the Tang Dynasty (618–907) brought wealth and stability to the empire. There was great social change during the 7th century as powerful positions were opened to educated men of humble birth and the old aristocracy was gradually replaced. Added to strong central government, these changes led to a golden age in the arts. Poets, painters, and other artists played an increasingly important role in cultural life.

This painting shows scholars sitting an official examination.

RISE OF TANG EMPIRE

618
Li Yuan (566–635) overthrows the last Sui emperor and establishes the Tang Dynasty, ruling as Emperor Gaozu.

626–649
Reign of Taizong, who expands the Chinese empire further west than ever before.

629–645
Pilgrim Xuanzang (602–664) travels to India and Southeast Asia, translating texts that further encourage Buddhism in China.

712–756
Reign of Xuanzong, a classic period of good government and flourishing of the arts.

747
Tang armies invade Bactria and Kashmir and defeat an Arab-Tibetan alliance. The conquest is reversed by Arabs in 751.

780
Three-volume Ch'a Ching ("Tea Classic") includes descriptions of formal tea ceremonies.

868
Production of the Diamond Sutra, the world's first block-printed book.

904–907
Reign of the last Tang emperor, Zhaoxuan.

Lutes such as this were of Persian origin. They were presented as gifts to foreign envoys visiting China.

Court and Capital

Under the Tang emperors, the imperial capital at Chang'an grew to become a great cultural center and one of the largest cities in the world. Artists, scholars, and merchants visited from many other countries. Life at the Tang court was a luxurious display of imperial power and artistic talent. A palace garden was reserved for training musicians and dancers, who performed at imperial ceremonies.

Political Expansion

Tang emperors expanded the use of examinations in culture and literature for hiring civil servants. This allowed educated men without family connections to show their true ability and get jobs as government officials. These officials formed an important link between the imperial court and local regions of the Empire.

THE TANG DYNASTY

The Tang Empire
Tang emperors extended Chinese control into Tibet and central Asia, but many 7th-century conquests were quickly overturned. The empire's neighbors, including Silla and Bohai in the northeast, adopted many aspects of Chinese life and government. Tang rulers promoted trade, and merchants went as far as Persia and Europe along the Silk Road. They carried silk, porcelain, tea, and other goods on trade routes, and brought wool and precious metals to China.

BOHAI
JAPAN
SILLA
TAIYUAN
CHANG'AN LUOYANG
EAST CHINA SEA
TIBET
INDIA
KHMER
CHAMPA
PHILIPPINES
CEYLON
BORNEO

Under temporary Tang control   Tang Empire   — Trade route   — Area of Chinese cultural influence

This Tang period gilded silver storage container for tea is decorated with bird designs.

Tea

During the Tang period tea drinking developed into an art form. Producers steamed and crushed the leaves and tea was sold in brick form. The drink was made by breaking a piece off and boiling it. Connoisseurs included scholars and officials. Special teas were cultivated for use at the imperial court, where elaborate tea ceremonies were introduced.

Above: This mural of courtly ladies in an imperial prince's tomb dates from 706.

Statuette of a woman on horseback. Tang women rode, hunted, and played polo.

Women

The great cultural and economic changes of the Tang period affected the lives of women, who were able to take a more active part in social life. More women learned to read and write, and many gained access to family property. Wu Zetian was one of the most remarkable women in Chinese history, ruling as empress from 690 to 705. She was a tough, skilful ruler, who chose advisers and officials for their ability rather than their social standing.

This monumental statue of Maitreya, the Buddha of the Future, was commissioned by Empress Wu Zetian. It still stands at the Longmen caves in present-day Hénán province.

The Song Dynasty

The first emperor of the Song Dynasty came to power in 960. The early period of the dynasty's rule, until 1126, is known as the Northern Song. During this time the imperial capital was at Kaifeng.

After the fall of this city to nomadic invaders the capital was moved south and the dynasty is known as the Southern Song. During the 300 years of Song rule great progress was made in farming methods, technology and the arts.

The first paper money was printed in 1024, after economic growth led to an increased demand for heavy coins.

Economic Growth

During the Song period a new kind of early-ripening rice was introduced in the southern region. This made it possible to grow two or even three crops a year, and efficient farming expanded food production. Population grew and cities flourished along the main waterways and southeast coast. Guilds were formed in the region as the number of tradespeople and artisans grew.

Unfired pottery called greenware, such as this ewer, was popular in the late Tang and early Five Dynasties period.

Before the Song

The last Tang emperor was toppled in 907, after provincial governors had broken away from central imperial government. Over the next 50 years, the empire went through a period of confusion and disunity, during which a series of different rulers fought for control. This troubled period (907–960) is known as the Five Dynasties and Ten Kingdoms.

Emperor Taizu

The Song Dynasty was founded in 960 by Zhao Kuangyin, who ended many years of regional power when he came to the throne as Emperor Taizu. Previously, members of the Song family had been officials in the northern region. Taizu proved to be an able administrator. He reorganized the government and the army, replacing provincial military governors with civilians. He was succeeded by his younger brother, Taizong.

A 10th-century portrait on silk of Emperor Taizu.

A busy street scene in the Northern Song capital of Kaifeng. Some passers-by stop and listen to a public storyteller, who may also have sung songs and told jokes.

Printing

In about 1045, a Chinese printer named Bi Sheng invented the world's first movable-type system. He carved individual characters in clay and fired them, before placing them in a tray. After printing, the clay blocks could be taken out and rearranged to make a different text. The new system was not readily adopted because Chinese writing has thousands of characters and it was easier to save and use unmovable wood-block pages.

Clay-block characters were wedged into an iron frame (1) and then coated with ink made from soot mixed with gum (2). Paper was placed on the inked characters and rubbed down with a pad (3). This transferred the characters to the paper (4).

This poem was written in 1082 by the great calligrapher and poet, Su Shi.

Song Culture

Song scholars developed a new way of thinking, which we call Neo-Confucianism. Their philosophy combined traditional Confucian morals with Buddhist and Taoist beliefs. The greatest Neo-Confucian master was the classical scholar Zhu Xi (1130–1200). Education was also strongly influenced by poetry, which was often sung to music.

In this 11th-century painting, a poet-calligrapher waits for inspiration.

THE SONG DYNASTY

907–960
Five dynasties rule a disunited empire.

960–976
Reign of Taizu, first emperor of the Song Dynasty.

1037–1101
Life of the great poet Su Shi, writing under the pen name Su Tungpo, whose father and son were also writers.

1101–1125
Reign of Emperor Huizong, a painter and calligrapher, who founds an academy of painting on the model of a Confucian college.

1126
The Song capital of Kaifeng falls to Jin invaders from Manchuria. The imperial capital is moved south to Hangzhou.

1234
The northern Jin Empire is conquered by the Mongols.

1279
The last Song emperor, six-year-old Bing Di, drowns in a sea battle against the Mongols.

This painting of bullocks was made on silk by the famous Chang'an artist Han Huang (723–787).

Below: A Tibetan envoy (far left) arrives at the court of Taizong (seated on a sedan).

Dry-lacquer statue of Jianzhen (688–763), a Chinese Buddhist monk who was invited by the Japanese emperor to train his own Buddhist teachers. Those traveling with Jianzhen introduced Chinese religious sculpture to Japan.

Conquest

The stability of the empire was founded on military strength and conquest. The armies of Taizong (reigned 626–649), son of the Tang founder Gaozu, forced Turkish nomads from the northern region of the empire and conquered parts of Tibet and Turkestan. After some of this territory was later lost, Empress Wu Zetian sent troops and reconquered it. As well as gaining territory, these conquests protected trade routes and promoted cultural exchange.

Artistic Exchange

The Tang period set very high standards for poetry, painting, and sculpture. Artistic skills were taken to the outlying cities and monasteries of the empire by traveling scholars and monks. A growing cultural exchange with neighboring lands included Japan, where Chinese technology and artistic themes, such as landscape painting, also spread.

Foreign Affairs

The Tang period marked a high point in relations with foreign powers. Tang culture and administration were admired beyond the empire, and Chinese civilization spread throughout East Asia. Neighboring countries such as present-day Korea, Japan, and Vietnam were strongly influenced. Foreign envoys regularly arrived at the Tang imperial court.

This mural shows Korean and other foreign ambassadors being received at the Tang court.

Chinese Influence in Asia

From Tang times, Chinese influence made itself felt throughout Asia. In the 7th century, Korean and Japanese rulers began introducing Chinese political practices, such as the division of territory into provincial regions. Buddhism was introduced from China to Japan, where rulers encouraged the new religion as a way of increasing imperial authority. The Chinese also used military conquest and trade as ways to expand their influence. Their cultural and technological advances traveled far beyond China.

Capital Cities

Tang methods of planning and construction were admired and copied by China's neighbors. The Japanese used the grid layout of Chang'an as a model for their capital at Nara in 710, and did the same again when the court moved to Heian in 794. In Korea, the Silla capital of Kyongju was expanded in a similar way, and the Silla kings soon adopted the Tang system of counties and prefectures.

The Tang city of Chang'an was based on a grid of broad avenues. There were great gates in its surrounding walls.

Trade Routes

Tang China grew into a great trading power, as the Silk Road increased traffic to the west. The Grand Canal was rebuilt and extended, linking the Chang Jiang (Yangtze River) with northern waterways including the Huang He (Yellow River). There was a road along the canal's embankments, with regular staging posts, repair workshops and storage warehouses. Only one Tang port, Guangzhou, was allowed to trade with foreigners, but by the 11th century there were seven others.

Painted wooden figurine from the Tang period.

The construction of new roads and bridges in China helped to increase trade and speed up the exchange of ideas and technology.

THE NOMADIC INVASIONS

907–926
Reign of the Liao Dynasty founder Abaoji.

907–1125
The Liao Dynasty rules over northeastern China.

1004
The Khitan attack Song Kaifeng and are paid tribute in silver and silk.

1117
The Jurchen invade Khitan territory.

1125–1234
Reign of the Jin Dynasty.

1206
Temujin is proclaimed Chingis Khan, supreme ruler of the Mongols.

1211
The Mongols force the Jin to move their capital from Beijing to Kaifeng.

1226
Chingis Khan is succeeded by his son Ogodei.

1232
The Mongols and the Southern Song unite to attack the Jin.

The Mongol Invasion

The northern borders of the Chinese empire were threatened by a succession of nomadic invaders. The attacks were begun by Khitan tribes, who formed their own Jin Dynasty early in the 10th century. They were followed 200 years later by Jurchen tribes and in the 13th century by the Mongols, who were united under the leadership of Chingis Khan. The Mongols built a vast empire across Asia, which included China after the collapse of the Song Dynasty.

A Khitan noble huntsman with his Mongolian horse.

The Khitan and Jurchen

The semi-nomadic people known as the Khitan were based in the Liao valley of Manchuria. At the beginning of the 10th century, a Khitan chieftain united several tribes into a federation and formed the Liao Dynasty, making Yenjing (Beijing) their southern capital. Early in the 12th century, a Jurchen clansman named Aguda formed a federation of his nomadic tribes. They broke away from the Liao Empire and formed the Jin Dynasty. The Jurchen first defeated the Liao and then turned on the Song Empire to the south.

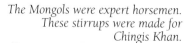

The Mongols were expert horsemen. These stirrups were made for Chingis Khan.

A Mongol horseman overlooks the group of yurts that make up his tribe's camp.

THE MONGOL EMPIRE

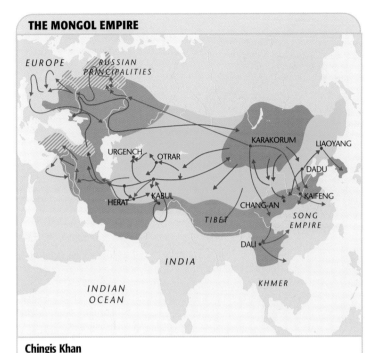

Chingis Khan

Temujin (c. 1167–1227) was the son of a Mongol chieftain. He took the name Chingis Khan, meaning "supreme ruler", when he united the separate Mongol tribes. Chingis Khan set about conquering lands with his fierce army of horsemen and succeeded in forming a vast empire. He established order throughout his empire and created a code of laws that suited his nomadic people.

→ Campaigns of Chingis Khan	Conquests of Chingis Khan 1209–1227	Mongol lands c. 1206
→ Mongol campaigns 1228–1260	Mongol conquests 1228–1260	Area of loose Mongol control

Dressed to Kill

The nomadic Mongols were superb soldiers and fighters naturally adapted to mobile warfare. Their clothing had to be very strong and hardwearing. Mongol warriors wore quilted tunics covered with ox-hide leather strips or iron scales for extra protection against enemy weapons. Soldiers were well equipped with spare clothing, weapons, tools and food, which they carried in a large hide saddlebag.

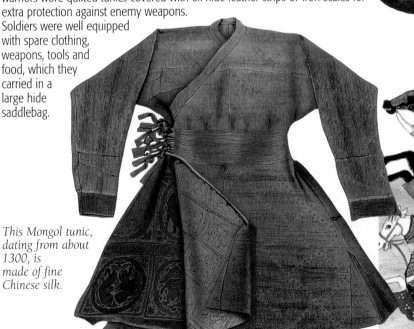

This Mongol tunic, dating from about 1300, is made of fine Chinese silk.

The Mongol Tribes

The Mongols were nomads who travelled the grasslands of central Asia with their herds of sheep and goats. They lived in scattered groups and moved around in constant search of new pastures for their animals. They took with them portable felt tents, called yurts, which gave good protection from the cold winds of the northern plains.

Gilded silver Khitan crown, decorated in a Chinese style.

Military Might

The Mongols were mighty conquerors and their strong, swift tactics instilled great fear in the people they attacked. Their warriors used superb horsemanship to overcome their enemies with speed and surprise. The Mongols were skilled bowmen, and they used battleaxes, lances and swords in close combat.

Miniature Buddhist pagoda made of gold and silver from the period of the Liao Dynasty.

The Mongols attacked in large numbers with great ferocity.

Mongol Rule

Following the Mongol invasions, the Yuan Dynasty ruled China from 1279 to 1368. Although the Mongols were harsh rulers, they interfered with traditional Chinese ways only when they felt they had to. They allowed a variety of religions among the Chinese people, including Buddhism and Taoism. At first, they were less sure of Confucian principles, but they recognized the value and importance of Confucian scholars and officials among the Chinese. Muslims from the west were also welcomed in the empire, where the development of drama and painting were encouraged.

Yuan Dynasty

In 1271, Khubilai Khan declared himself "Emperor of China," although the Southern Song were not finally defeated until eight years later. The new dynasty was named Yuan, meaning "great originator" in Chinese. The Yuan capital of Dadu (Beijing) was laid out like a Chinese city, and the emperor allowed his Chinese subjects to rule themselves, under Mongol supervision.

A stoneware jar from the Yuan period.

Khubilai Khan

Khubilai (1215–1294) was the grandson of Chingis Khan. The Mongols completed their conquest of China under his leadership, and he became the first foreigner to rule over a united Chinese empire. Khubilai allowed religious freedom and gained the reputation of being a humane ruler. He extended the Grand Canal between the Yellow River and his capital Dadu, and improved Chinese roads.

MONGOLS IN CHINA

1254–1322
Life of the great Chinese painter Zhao Mengfu, who was descended from a Song emperor.

1275
Venetian merchant Marco Polo (c. 1254–1324) arrives in China.

1279–1294
Reign of Khubilai Khan, first ruler of the Yuan Dynasty.

1333–1368
Reign of Toghon Temur, longest-ruling and last Yuan emperor.

1353–1354
Outbreak of Black Death (plague) in China.

1361–1405
Rule of Timur in Samarkand.

1368
Zhu Yuanzhang, founder of the Ming Dynasty, captures Dadu (Beijing).

This painting by Zhao Mengfu is dated 1296, two years after Khubilai's death.

Bronze portrait of Timur, who was a devout Muslim.

Timur

The great Mongol general and conqueror Timur, or Tamerlane (1336–1405), claimed to be descended form Chingis Khan. He was born near Samarkand (in present-day Uzbekistan), the son of the leader of a Turkic-speaking Mongol tribe. Timur invaded India, defeated the Ottoman Turks and was on an expedition to China when he died.

Right: Bronze disks such as this were carried by Mongol envoys on official imperial business. The disk acted as a kind of passport.

Women of the Period

In nomadic Mongol society women were often responsible for looking after livestock. Some Mongol women even took part in warfare, though this was the prime responsibility of all men. Women had the right to divorce and to own property themselves. Female members of the imperial family had great influence. An example was Khubilai's wife Chabi, who encouraged fair and humane treatment of the Song after their defeat by the Mongols.

Portrait of Chabi, Khubilai's second and favorite wife.

Cultured Court

Khubilai was a patron of the arts. The Mongol emperor supported Chinese painters, as well as craftsmen working in ceramics and fine textiles. This resulted in an improvement in the status of artisans during the Mongol period. One of the greatest painters of the time was Zhao Mengfu, who added poetic inscriptions to his works. Zhao received a position in Khubilai's court.

In 1281 Khubilai Khan tried to invade the islands of Japan. But the Mongols sailed into a typhoon, which destroyed their fleet. The Japanese thought they were saved by a kamikaze or "divine wind."

Asuka and Nara Japan

The islands of Japan had strong links with the mainland of East Asia, especially China and Korea. It was from there that writing, farming, a new religion, and a system of government reached Japan. In 552, the Buddhist religion spread from Korea. This key event marked the start of Japan's Asuka period (552–645), named after the region on the island of Honshu. Japanese culture began to flourish, setting a pattern for future periods.

Changes in Society

Japanese society underwent many great changes. Prince Shotoku (574–622) created Japan's first constitution, designed to bring order to society. After his death, the Taika Reforms brought more changes from the 640s onwards. Japan's rulers based the changes on Chinese ones. The emperor—Japan's ultimate ruler—grew in power, not the clan chieftains. Taxes were collected from the peasantry, new laws were introduced, as was a postal service, and Buddhism was actively promoted.

A wooden mask, made in the 700s, worn by a Japanese actor in a drama at a Buddhist temple.

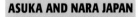

ASUKA AND NARA JAPAN

552–645
The Asuka period.

552
Buddhism introduced to Japan from Korea.

600s
Changes in society are begun by Prince Shotoku. Chinese-style government comes to Japan.

645
Soga clan slip from power and the Asuka period ends.

646
The Taika Reforms begin, in which the emperor becomes the supreme leader.

710–794
The Nara period.

710
Heijokyo (Nara) becomes first permanent capital, modeled on the Chinese city of Chang'an.

712
Japan's first history is written.

794
Nara period ends and capital moves to Heiankyo (modern Kyoto).

A million of these small wooden miniatures of stupas (sacred burial mounds or structures) were made in the Nara period, each with a Buddhist prayer of thanks inside.

The Nara Period

After the Asuka period, Japan's next highpoint was the Nara period (710–794). It was in this time that Heijokyo (present-day Nara, after which the period is named) became the capital city (see opposite), Buddhism became the official religion, the emperor emerged as the head of state, and arts, crafts, and architecture flourished. Links with China remained strong, and Chinese influence was felt throughout Japanese society.

Raising Taxes

As society grew more centralized, with a state government, there was a greater need to collect taxes from the people. Peasants paid their taxes to the state as a percentage of what they grew (such as rice), or in textiles, labor, or military service. Their taxes were handed over at government stations along Japan's excellent road network. High taxes meant poverty for many peasants.

Wooden tags were fixed to goods that had been collected as taxes for the state.

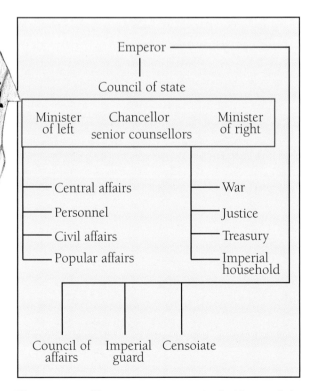

The structure of Japanese government in the Nara period.

Japan's first coins were made in the early 700s. The idea of coinage came to Japan from China.

Many Capitals
Until the 700s, a new capital was built each time a new ruler came to the throne (to avoid being "polluted" by the old ruler's death). Japan's early capitals were in the west of Honshu island, where Japanese civilization began. As society became more sophisticated, the first permanent capital was established at Heijokyo (modern Nara), in 710. Laid out on a grid pattern, some 3 miles (5 km) square, Heijokyo was home to 100,000 people.

The main temple in the Horyu-ji temple complex, the Golden Hall, was built between 670 and 714 by carpenters from Korea.

Lecture Hall

Golden Hall

Pagoda

Inner Gate

Plan of the Horyu-ji Buddhist temple complex at Heijokyo (Nara).

Prince Shotoku in prayer to the Buddha. He is the "patron saint" of Japanese Buddhism.

Warrior Clans of Japan
Japanese society was ruled by warrior families, or clans, each headed by a powerful chieftain. In the late 500s, the Soga clan, supporters of Buddhism, defeated rivals opposed to this "foreign" religion. The Soga became Japan's rulers, and Prince Shotoku, a member of the clan, set about changing Japanese society. He helped spread Buddhism and established links with China. After his death, the Soga struggled for control, losing their hold on power in 645.

Heian Period in Japan

In 794, Emperor Kammu moved the capital of Japan from Heijokyo (Nara) to a new city at Heiankyo (modern Kyoto). He ordered the move because of concerns that Buddhism, well established in Heijokyo, was starting to affect the government. Moving the capital was Kammu's way of starting again. Heiankyo was home to some 100,000 people. The city gave its name to a new period in Japanese history—the Heian period (794–1185).

Bronze figure of Zao Gongen, a mountain spirit worshipped in the Heian period.

Above: A court official, seated at the right, is sent into exile by the Fujiwara clan. This was the fate of those who dared to question their rule.

The Fujiwara Clan

Japan's clans continued to co-exist with the emperor. They were closely connected, and while the emperor sought to increase his power, the clans did all they could to influence him. The leading clan in the Heian period was the Fujiwara. Its daughters married into the royal family, and the Fujiwara became the true power in Japan. The emperor's powers faded.

HEIAN PERIOD

781
Start of Emperor Kammu's reign, in the late Nara period.

794
Heian period begins when Emperor Kammu moves the capital to Heiankyo (Kyoto).

806
Death of Emperor Kammu.

c. 1010
Murasaki Shikibu writes The Tale of Genji.

1134
A huge storm sweeps away many houses in Heiankyo.

1150s–1180s
Civil war between rival clans leads to the end of the Fujiwara clan's control.

1177
One third of Heiankyo is destroyed by fire.

1181
Famine strikes Heiankyo and 20,000 people starve to death.

1185
The Heian period ends.

HEIAN JAPAN

SEA OF JAPAN

HEIANKYO (KYOTO)

HONSHU

HEIJOKYO (NARA)

SHIKOKU

KYUSHU

PACIFIC OCEAN

Minamoto Yoshinaka, 1183
Minamoto Yoritomo, 1183
Northern Fujiwara, 1183
Taira, 1183
● Capital city
♟ Estates of the Fujiwara (9th–12th centuries)
Furthest extent of Yoritomo territory, 1189

Warrior Clans in Heian Japan

Japan's imperial power structure, with the emperor as the supreme head of state, declined after the death of Emperor Kammu in 806. As the position of emperor lost its power, so the warrior class gained in strength. Major battles were fought in which power was steadily won by leading military families. The warrior clans took control of parts of the country, ruling them as independent feudal states. In the battle of Heiji (1158) the Heike clan emerged as the most powerful family. In turn, the Heike lost power to the Genji clan, who defeated them in the battle of Dan no Ura (1185).

Japanese potters of the Heian period produced high quality vases, such as this large jar.

Emperor, Chieftains, Nobles, and Peasants

Japan's government became increasingly complicated in the Heian period. The emperor tried to control the nation's five million people by dividing the country into 66 provinces, each with a governor and hundreds of officials. Added to this were the warrior clans, such as the Fujiwara, who influenced the emperor's decisions. They were the "power behind the throne." Then there were rich land-owning nobles who did as they pleased. At the bottom of society were the poor peasants who made up the bulk of the population.

Literature and the World's First Novel

Japan's first great works of fiction and poetry were written in the Heian period. Much of it was by aristocratic women at the court of the emperor. The leading female writer was Murasaki Shikibu (c. 978–1014), often known as "Lady Murasaki." Her *Genji monogatari* (The Tale of Genji), written in about 1010, is considered the world's first novel. It is the story of Prince Genji, and describes life at the emperor's court.

Murasaki Shikibu writing her novel, The Tale of Genji. The story was written in installments which were eagerly consumed by aristocratic female readers.

This fan is decorated with hand-painted scenes of servants cleaning the entrance to a temple.

The Arts Flourish

Religious and secular (non-religious) art flourished in the Heian period. Religious art was connected with Buddhism, and also with the traditional Japanese Shinto religion. Artists carved statues in wood, and produced scrolls decorated with finely painted scenes of landscapes and people. They transformed everyday objects, such as mirrors, wooden boxes, and games boards into works of art, covering them with layers of shiny lacquer or inlaying them with mother-of-pearl.

This wooden figure of a lion, carved in the 1100s, originally stood guard at a temple.

Buddha riding on a white elephant, representing the soul of Buddha, painted on an Heian scroll.

Japan Under the Shoguns

THE SHOGUNATES

1159–1160
Heiki war, fought between rival clans the Heiki and the Minamoto, which the Heiki win.

1180–1185
Gempei war, fought between the Heiki and the Minamoto, which the Minamoto win.

1185
Kamakura period begins.

1192
Minamoto Yoritomo (born 1147) appointed Japan's first shogun; a new form of government begins.

1199
Minamoto Yoritomo dies.

1232
A new code of law is introduced, strengthening the shoguns' powers.

1274 and 1281
Japanese armies defeat Mongol invasions from China.

1333
Kamakura period ends after a rebellion; a new family rise to power as the next shoguns.

In the late 1100s, a great change took place in Japan when control of the country shifted away from the emperor and the nobility and into the hands of military chieftains or dictators. The first of these dictators was Minamoto Yoritomo. In 1192, he forced the emperor—a boy aged 13—to give him the title of shogun ("great general"). For the next 700 years, Japan came under the rule of the shoguns.

This wooden saddle, made in the 1200s, is inlaid with mother-of-pearl decoration.

Samurai–Japan's Ultimate Warriors

Of all Japan's warriors, none was more respected–or feared–than the samurai. These professional warriors first appeared in the 800s. By the 1200s, the samurai had become the most powerful warriors in the land, armed with swords, lances, and bows. They followed a warrior code called *bushido* ("the warrior's way") which was made up of strict rules. The most important rule was to defend the noble they worked for.

Samurai fought with lances, but their main weapons were their swords, which were often of superb quality.

Feudal Society

During the period of the shoguns, Japan had a feudal society. Under feudalism all land was owned by the shogun and leading families. The country's peasants, who formed the bulk of the population, worked on the land as tenants, producing goods for their landlords. Inevitably, the landlords were rich, but the peasants were poor.

Shogun Government

Before the shoguns took control, the country's government had been similar to that of China, with the emperor as leader. All this changed when Minamoto Yoritomo came to power as shogun. He moved the capital from Heiankyo (Kyoto) to a new center at Kamakura, 30 miles (50 km) south of present-day Tokyo. The emperor was allowed to remain in Heiankyo, where he was a figurehead without power. Minamoto Yoritomo reorganized the country. He introduced a new style of government with military governors to rule over the country's many landholding magnates, the daimyo.

JAPAN UNDER SHOGUN CONTROL

— Borders, 1467

▮ *Daimyo* territories

♟ Shogun capital

SEA OF JAPAN

ASHIKAGA 1338–1573

KAMAKURA 1185–1333

HONSHU

SHIKOKU

PACIFIC OCEAN

KYUSHU

The Family in Japanese Society

It was normal for several generations of the same family to live in one house, with the oldest man as head of the household. Children were brought up to show respect for their elders, and everyone in the family was expected to set good standards of behavior. Women were seen as less important than men. They had to obey men, and women in noble families were rarely seen in public.

Wealthy Japanese women wore a kimono—a long coat with short sleeves, tied at the waist with a sash. Samurai-class women wore a large, flowing garment called an uchikaka over their kimonos.

Civil Wars Between Warrior Clans

In Japan's feudal society there was constant tension between the clans. As their wealth increased, the clans formed private armies. By the mid-1100s the greatest warrior clans were the Heike and the Minamoto, who fought a civil war in 1159. The Heike won, but, 20 years later, were defeated by the Minamoto. From this second civil war the Minamoto leader, Yoritomo (1147–1199), emerged as Japan's first shogun leader.

A sculpture from a temple, believed to depict Minamoto Yoritomo.

Above: an armorer ties together the strips of leather in a suit of armor, which was designed for ease of movement in combat.

KOREA

Before 660
*Period of the
Three Kingdoms.*

660
*Munmu Wang of Silla
(reigned 661–681) defeats
the kingdom of Paekche.*

668
*Munmu Wang defeats
the kingdom of Goguryeo.
He is first ruler of a
unified Korea.*

668–935
Unified Silla period.

698–926
Parhae kingdom period.

935
Koryo Kingdom begins.

1231–1257
*Period of Mongol invasions
from China.*

1231
*Koryo court flees
to an island base.*

1270
*Peace treaty signed with
the Mongol invaders.*

1388
*Mongols lose power
in China.*

1392
Koryo Kingdom ends.

First Ruler of All Korea

The kingdom of Silla, in southeastern Korea, was one of the three big Korean kingdoms. In the 660s, the king of Silla, Munmu Wang, was helped by China to conquer the other two major kingdoms. Munmu Wang became the first ruler of all Korea. The years that followed, from 668 to 935, are known as the Unified Silla period. At this time Korea was one state, not a group of kingdoms.

Korean roof tile, from about 800, decorated with a monster to keep evil spirits away.

The Koryo Kingdom

After nearly 270 years of rule by the kings of Unified Silla, civil war brought the period to an end. In 935, a new kingdom emerged to dominate Korea—Goryeo, also known as Koryo (from which comes the English name for Korea). The Koryo period was a rich one, particularly for arts and religion. Potters excelled in making high-quality vases and Buddhism became the national religion. A rebellion brought the period to an end in 1392.

The Parhae Kingdom

Munmu Wang's defeat of the kingdom of Goguryeo in 668 meant that he became ruler of all Korea. A general from Goguryeo led his defeated people into exile. In 698, the exiled Goguryeo people established the kingdom of Parhae, in the far north of Korea. Parhae was on friendly terms with Unified Silla, which controlled the Korean peninsula to the south.

Statue of Buddha, made in Korea in the 700s from bronze and gold leaf.

The Kingdoms of Korea

Several advanced cultures developed on the peninsula of Korea. Each had its own individual characteristics, and the territory it controlled was its kingdom. In the early centuries of Korean history, there were three major rival kingdoms that fought each other. As a result of the conflict, new kingdoms were born, and in the 10th century Korea entered a period of relative calm in which the arts flourished.

The Buddhist Temple of the Floating Stone was founded in 676, in the reign of King Munmu Wang of Silla. The present building dates from 1358.

An illustration painted in gold by a Korean Buddhist monk in 1341. It forms two pages from a book about the Buddha.

KINGDOM OF KOREA

LIAOYANG

ANBUK

PYONGYANG

KAEGYONG
SEOUL

PUYU

KYONGJU

YELLOW SEA

— Border of the Three Kingdoms, c. 350–688
— Kingdom of the Parhae, 694–926
— Kingdom of Silla, 676–c. 900
→ Chinese invasion, 660–668
→ Mongol invasion, 1231–1254
▉ Kingdom of Koryu c. 960
■ Koryu border fort

Mongol Invasions of Korea
In the early 1200s, the Koryo Kingdom came under pressure from the Mongols, who had entered China and taken control of much of the country. In 1231, the Mongols invaded Koryo, and for the next 30 years struggled to conquer the kingdom. The two sides signed a peace treaty in 1270, which lasted until 1388, when the Mongols were ousted from China by native Chinese. This unrest affected Koryo. Some leaders remained friendly with the Mongols, but others preferred to make links with China's new rulers. The court of Koryo was split, leading to its collapse in 1392.

Korean Pottery
The world's first pottery was made in Asia, where potters worked hard to perfect their craft, particularly in Japan, China, and Korea. Korean pottery reached a highpoint in the Koryo period, especially in the range of different shapes produced and the use of glazes. Korean glazes of this period gave the surface of pots a smooth finish, usually in shades of pale green. Glazed pots were expensive items. For everyday use, unglazed stone pots were used.

Glazed stoneware vase from the 1100s, decorated with a willow tree. It was used for serving wine.

Fumes escaped through the holes in this stoneware incense burner, made in the shape of a lotus flower.

As a glaze cooled, it shrank a little, producing a crackled effect that was much admired, as on this plate.

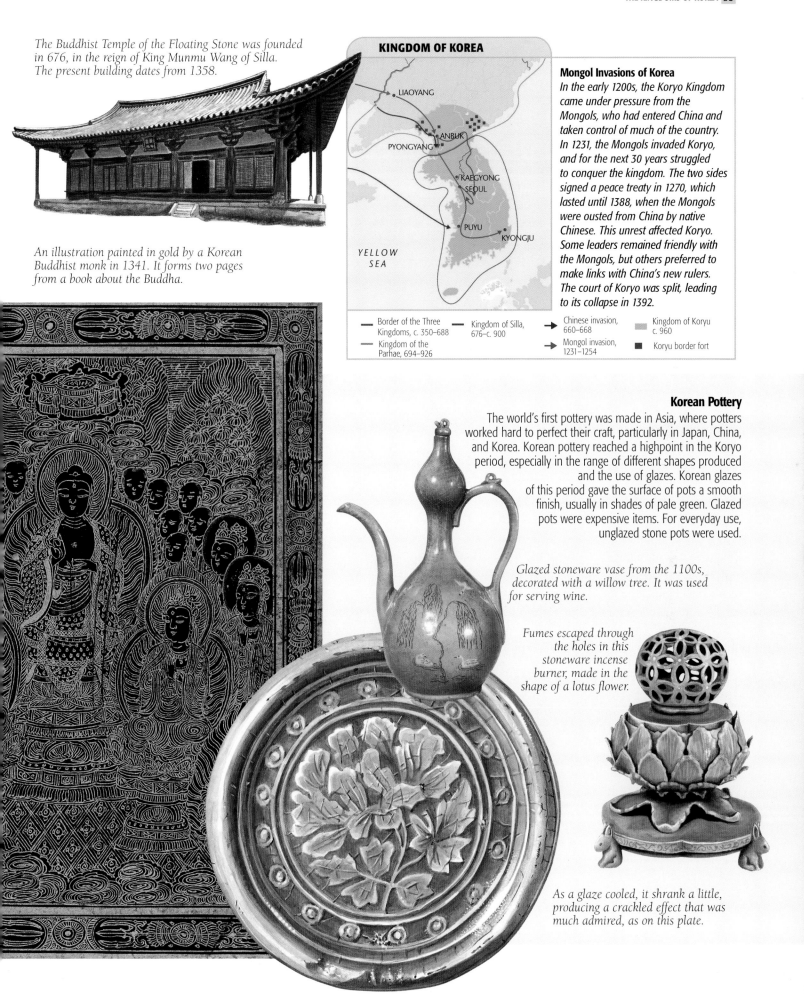

SOUTHEAST ASIA

192–1697
Cham Kingdom period in Vietnam.

602
Rebellion in Vietnam crushed by China.

802–1432
Khmer kingdom period in Cambodia.

850–1287
Burmese kingdom period in Myanmar.

1177
Khmer capital at Angkor briefly captured by the Chams.

1258–1293
Start of Mongol incursions into Southeast Asia.

1287
Burmese capital at Pagan sacked by the Mongols.

1292–1558
Chiang Mai kingdom period in Thailand.

1440
Angkor abandoned by the Khmers.

People unable to read learned about Buddhism from pictures like this.

Both sides of a tiny gold cube used as currency on Java, Indonesia, in the 800s. One side has a letter, the other a symbol. Each mark shows links with Hindu India.

Cash coin from Vietnam. The hole allowed it to be carried on a string for easy counting, often in units of 100 coins.

Common Currency

Coins from China and Southeast Asia were similar in design. Known as "cash" coins (from a Tamil word for a small coin), they were round with a square hole in the center and four Chinese characters on the front. First made in China in the 500s BCE, the design of these copper alloy coins was widely copied. They had a standard value and were accepted across the region.

Southeast Asian Kingdoms

Between the years 500 and 800, many small kingdoms emerged on the mainland of Southeast Asia. By 1000, they had given way to larger kingdoms and empires, the greatest of which was centered on Cambodia. This was the home of the powerful Khmer, who built a magnificent capital at Angkor. Other states flourished across the region, each with a distinctive identity.

Kingdom of the Cham

The kingdom of people known as the Cham lay in the south and centre of Vietnam. It came into existence in 192 CE, after a Cham lord rebelled against the Chinese who had controlled the area until then. The Cham kingdom lasted for about 1,500 years, until the late 1600s. It was influenced by Indian culture—most of the population were Hindus, and the varna social system was adopted, in which people were ranked according to their place in society (see page 39).

Stone sculpture of a guardian dragon, made in the kingdom of the Cham in about 1200.

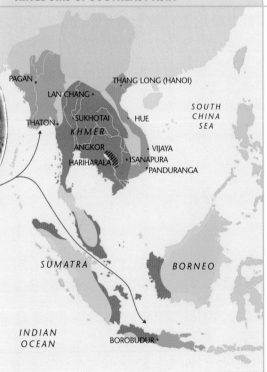

KINGDOMS OF SOUTHEAST ASIA

PAGAN
THANG LONG (HANOI)
LAN CHANG
SUKHOTAI • HUE
THATON • *KHMER*
SOUTH CHINA SEA
ANGKOR • VIJAYA
HARIHARALA • ISANAPURA
PANDURANGA
SUMATRA
BORNEO
INDIAN OCEAN
BOROBUDUR

States and Kingdoms
Southeast Asia, with its many island groups, saw numerous cultures rise and fall in the period between 500 and 1500. For those that developed across Java, Sumatra, and Malaysia, trade networks were established over the surrounding seas. Contact between the cultures, particularly with India, helped to spread religion, art, and architecture across this vast region.

Stateless farming people
Nan Chao c. 600–1253
Pagan, c. 850–1287
Minor Hindu/ Buddhist states
Kediri, c. 1050–1225
Srivijaya influence, c. 600–1280
Annan/Dai Viet, 939–1885
Core of Khmer influence, 802
Champa, 192–1720
Chola raids, 1017–1068

The Burmese Kingdom

Many cultures established themselves in Myanmar (Burma). Among the first were the Mon and the Pyu peoples, who created small Buddhist kingdoms in the valley of the Irrawaddy River. Between 500 and 950, Burman people migrated into Myanmar. They established a base at Pagan, and by 850 the city was the capital of a Burmese kingdom. It lasted until 1287, when Mongols overran the city, bringing the kingdom to an end.

Bronze statue coated with gold leaf of a Khmer king. It depicts him as a god.

The Khmer Empire

The Khmer Empire, based in Cambodia, extended across much of present-day Laos, Thailand and Vietnam. It began in 802, when King Jayavarman II was declared "king of the world." He founded a dynasty of rulers who established their capital at Angkor, a vast city of temples where a million people lived. In 1177, Angkor was briefly taken by the Cham of Vietnam. The empire began to collapse and, under pressure from Vietnam and Thailand, it ceased to exist by the early 1400s.

Cham prisoners, tied at the neck, are led away by the Khmer, who ride elephants and horses.

The Buddhist temple of Ananda at Pagan, Myanmar, dates from 1105.

Dancing nature spirits known as Apsaras, from a carved panel at Angkor, Cambodia.

Art and Architecture

The styles of Southeast-Asian art and architecture are linked to those of India and China. This is due to the cultural influence from these countries, which brought with it "correct" ways to depict gods and goddesses and build places of worship. Amongst the crafts, such as pottery-making, lacquerware, ivory-carving, and work with semi-precious stones, the influence of China was felt. Manufacturing techniques from China were learned by the workers of Southeast Asia, who applied them to the objects they made.

The New Religions of Southeast Asia

The Buddhist and Hindu religions spread to Southeast Asia from India and China, carried there by traders and missionaries in the period between 100 and 400 CE. As they took root, they replaced the region's traditional beliefs which were based on the worship of deities linked to nature. Hinduism, from India, established itself most strongly in Cambodia, Vietnam, and Indonesia (Java, Sumatra, Bali), while Buddhism, from China and India, became widespread across the region.

Statue of Ganesh, an elephant-headed Hindu god, carved in Cambodia or Thailand in the 900s.

Southeast Asian Culture

The cultures of Southeast Asia were strongly influenced by others. They accepted ideas from outside their region, learned to live with them and adapted them to their own needs. For Laos, Cambodia, Vietnam, Thailand, Myanmar (Burma), and the islands of Indonesia, new ideas arrived from two places—India and China. From here came the religions of Hinduism, Buddhism, and Islam, bringing new styles of art, craft, and architecture.

Merchants from Vietnam and Borneo taking gifts to the emperor of China. In return, they hoped the emperor would support their trading activities.

Islamic Influence

For a thousand years, Hinduism and particularly Buddhism flourished among the cultures of Southeast Asia. This began to change in the late 1300s, when Muslim traders from India and Arabia introduced the religion of Islam to the region. It first became established in the trading centers of Java and Sumatra, from where it spread to the other islands of Indonesia. By the 1500s, Islam had replaced Hinduism as the dominant religion in these places.

A pottery storage vase made in Thailand. Its shape and glaze are copied from Chinese vases.

Borobudur is decorated with 1.6 million carved stones. Its relief carvings stretch for 1.5 miles (2.5 km).

Borobudur is a massive step-pyramid more than 98 feet (30 m) high, consisting of nine rising terraces decorated with Buddha statues, reliefs and stupas.

Borobudur, Java

Standing on the summit of a low hill in central Java, Indonesia, is one of the world's greatest ancient monuments. The Buddhist shrine of Borobudur, built between the late 700s and 800s, was constructed as the ceremonial heart of a nearby monastery. A series of square and round terraces lead up to a central stupa. Hundreds of smaller stupas line the upper terraces. Carved stone panels line the lower terraces, showing scenes from Buddhist literature. Borobudur is a Buddhist model of the universe, with the carvings representing levels of wisdom and the central stupa symbolizing the Buddha himself.

There are more than 500 stone statues of Buddha at Borobudur, like the one shown here.

Borobudur is set upon a natural hill. With each step the pilgrims climb, they symbolically reach a higher level of spirituality.

Northern India and the Deccan

During the 300s and 400s, the Gupta Dynasty ruled much of India from their northern kingdom of Magadha. However, invasions by Asiatic tribes caused the Gupta Empire to collapse and India became a patchwork of small kingdoms. The northern kingdoms were briefly reunited under Harsha Vardhana, and those in the northwest formed a union of interrelated kingdoms in the region known as the Rajputana.

Seal from a document recording a grant of land in Gujarat, northwestern India.

The Harsha Period

By the mid-500s, northern India had become divided into many small kingdoms. They lacked leadership until a warrior-king, Harsha Vardhana (reigned 606–648) unified the region. Harsha forged a Buddhist empire from central India to the Himalayas, and outlawed the killing of any creature or the eating of any flesh within his empire. Harsha's short-lived empire collapsed after his death.

Prithviraj III, king of a Rajput dynasty, and ruler of a kingdom in northern India in the 1100s.

The Rajput Kingdoms of Northwest India

Between the 300s and 600s, Scythians and Huns from Eurasia settled in northern India, where they established kingdoms. Their descendants were the Rajputs, who rose to prominence in Rajputana ("country of the kings") during the 800s and 900s. One of the greatest Rajput kings was Prithviraj III (c. 1165–1192), who turned Chauhan into India's leading Hindu state. In 1191, Prithviraj repelled a Muslim army, but refused to destroy it when it was in retreat. His chivalry was his undoing. The Muslims returned to defeat Prithviraj a year later.

There are many temples at Khajuraho, each richly decorated on the outside with hundreds of carved figures of people and animals.

The main Hindu temple at Khajuraho, central India, was built around the year 1000.

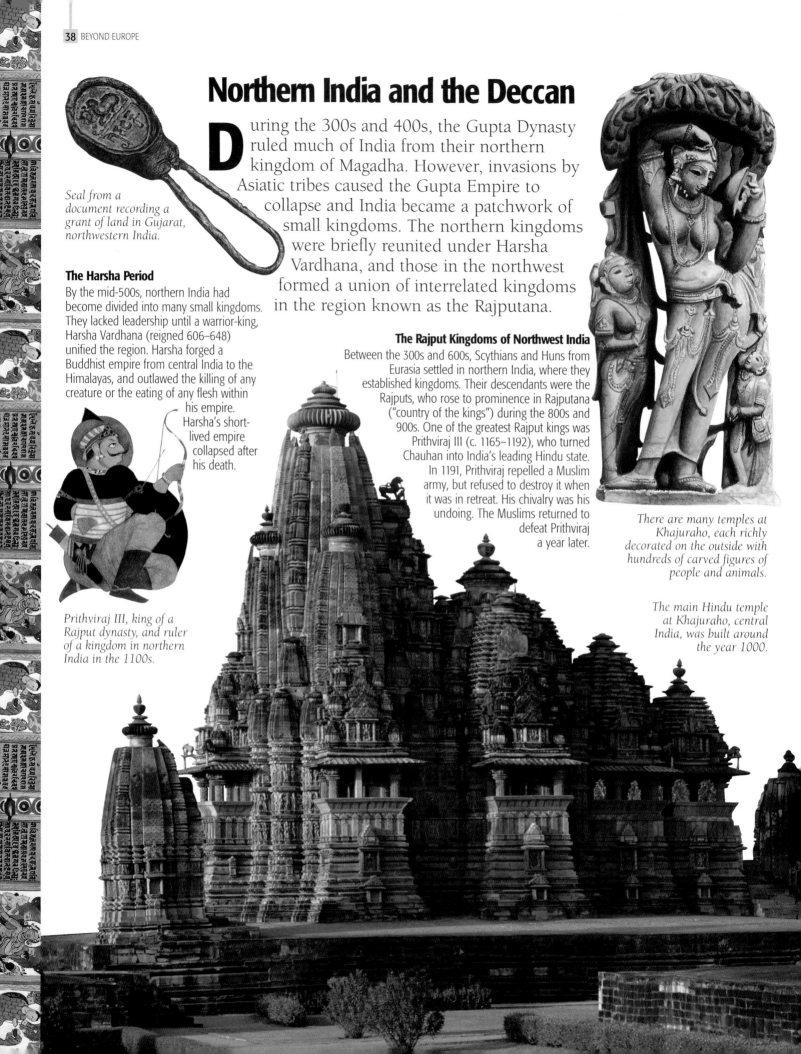

Struggle for Kannauj

The city of Kannauj was the capital of Harsha Vardhana's brief empire in northern India in the 600s (see opposite). It occupied a key location at the center of the Ganges River plain, the region's principal waterway. After the fall of the Harsha Empire, three rival states struggled to control Kannauj. Between the 800s and 1000s it was the capital of the Pratihara Empire, and was famous for its poets. However, in 1018 the city was taken by Turkish invaders, and its fortunes declined.

Bronze ewer and stand, made in the 1100s. It held sacred water, and was used in a Hindu temple.

Bronze figure of Lokeswar, the Buddhist Lord of the World. It was made in the 1100s.

Kingdoms of India

India has a diverse geography, from fertile river valleys and plains in the north, to the high rocky Deccan Plateau in the center and south. This geography influenced the development of Medieval kingdoms, effectively dividing them into northern and southern states, with no one group able to dominate the whole of the subcontinent.

INDIA IN c. 640

HAZNI · TIBET · Ganges River · DELHI · GURJARAS · KANNAUJ · GWALIOR · BENARES · UDAIPUR (MEWAR) · KHAJURAHO · DEOGIRI · CHALUKYAS · VATAPI · AIHOLE · BAY OF BENGAL · KANCHIPURAM · KOLKOI · MADURAI · ANURADHAPURA · POLONNARUWA

Harsha Empire

The Social System

In ancient India, a social system developed that grouped people into communities. India's earliest text, known as the *Rig Veda*, describes society as being divided into four large groups, that today are called varnas. At the very top of the system were the Brahmins, who were traditionally priests and teachers. Second were the Kshatriyas (kings, rulers, and warriors). Third were the Vaiyshas (landlords and businessmen), and the fourth were the Sudras (peasants and other workers). Each varna was divided into castes. Below the four varnas were people who were considered to be outsiders, sometimes called "untouchables." These people had degrading, dirty jobs such as cleaners and sewage workers.

A page of an Indian religious book, written on palm leaf paper in about 1065.

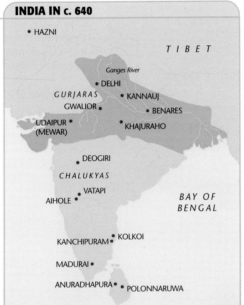
Ceiling decoration from a temple, made in the 700s, showing a ring of armed Kshatriya warriors.

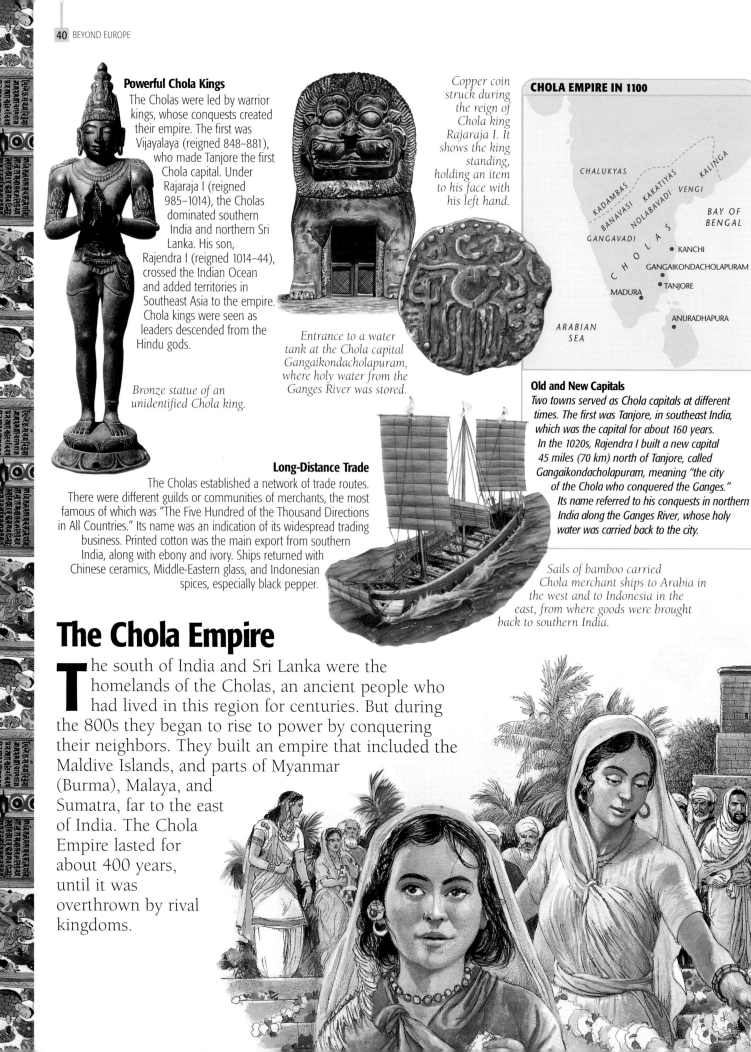

Powerful Chola Kings

The Cholas were led by warrior kings, whose conquests created their empire. The first was Vijayalaya (reigned 848–881), who made Tanjore the first Chola capital. Under Rajaraja I (reigned 985–1014), the Cholas dominated southern India and northern Sri Lanka. His son, Rajendra I (reigned 1014–44), crossed the Indian Ocean and added territories in Southeast Asia to the empire. Chola kings were seen as leaders descended from the Hindu gods.

Bronze statue of an unidentified Chola king.

Copper coin struck during the reign of Chola king Rajaraja I. It shows the king standing, holding an item to his face with his left hand.

Entrance to a water tank at the Chola capital Gangaikondacholapuram, where holy water from the Ganges River was stored.

CHOLA EMPIRE IN 1100

CHALUKYAS

KADAMBAS
BANAVASI
KAKATIYAS
NOLABAVADI VENGI
KALINGA

GANGAVADI

C H O L A S

BAY OF BENGAL

KANCHI

GANGAIKONDACHOLAPURAM

MADURA • TANJORE

ARABIAN SEA

ANURADHAPURA

Old and New Capitals

Two towns served as Chola capitals at different times. The first was Tanjore, in southeast India, which was the capital for about 160 years. In the 1020s, Rajendra I built a new capital 45 miles (70 km) north of Tanjore, called Gangaikondacholapuram, meaning "the city of the Chola who conquered the Ganges." Its name referred to his conquests in northern India along the Ganges River, whose holy water was carried back to the city.

Long-Distance Trade

The Cholas established a network of trade routes. There were different guilds or communities of merchants, the most famous of which was "The Five Hundred of the Thousand Directions in All Countries." Its name was an indication of its widespread trading business. Printed cotton was the main export from southern India, along with ebony and ivory. Ships returned with Chinese ceramics, Middle-Eastern glass, and Indonesian spices, especially black pepper.

Sails of bamboo carried Chola merchant ships to Arabia in the west and to Indonesia in the east, from where goods were brought back to southern India.

The Chola Empire

The south of India and Sri Lanka were the homelands of the Cholas, an ancient people who had lived in this region for centuries. But during the 800s they began to rise to power by conquering their neighbors. They built an empire that included the Maldive Islands, and parts of Myanmar (Burma), Malaya, and Sumatra, far to the east of India. The Chola Empire lasted for about 400 years, until it was overthrown by rival kingdoms.

Bronze figures of supernatural beings known as dakinis ("sky dancers"). They were believed to help Buddhists towards spiritual understanding.

Religion in Chola Society

The major religion in most of the Chola Empire was Hinduism. Chola kings built stone temples, lavishly decorated with images of the Hindu god Shiva. Other religions were tolerated, and worshipers were allowed to practice their beliefs. For example, Buddhism flourished on Sri Lanka. New branches of Buddhism appeared, such as Tantric Buddhism in which yoga and meditation were used by followers in their search for enlightenment.

A stone carving at a temple in southern India shows the Hindu god Shiva tying the turban of a worshiper.

THE CHOLAS

848–881
Reign of Vijayalaya, the first Chola king.

c. 850
Vijayalaya makes Tanjore the Chola capital.

897
Cholas conquer rival Pallavas.

Early 900s
Cholas conquer rival Pandyas.

c. 1000
Chola expedition to Sri Lanka returns to India with shiploads of loot.

1020s
Rajendra I makes Gangaikondacholapuram the new Chola capital.

1023
Rajendra I sends an expedition north to the Ganges River, and brings its holy water back to his new capital.

c. 1030
Cholas raid Southeast Asia.

Early 1200s
Chola Empire in southern India begins to shrink, as neighboring kingdoms take its land.

1246–1279
Reign of Rajendra IV, the last Chola king; the Chola Empire ends when he dies.

Temple Rituals

Temples were at the very centre of Chola society. These huge stone structures had open courtyards that were used as schools for the teaching of the Hindu religion. They gave shelter to the poor and medicine to the sick. As public meeting places, crowds walked in procession, carrying bronze statues of Hindu gods. The statues were skilfully made, and on their journey around their temple homes the faithful draped them in clothes, jewelry, and garlands of flowers.

Gangaikonda Temple, at the Chola's new capital, dates from c. 1050. Worshipers carried statues of Hindu gods around the building.

Southern India and Sri Lanka

Several kingdoms attempted to gain control of southern India and Sri Lanka between about 500 and 1000. It was a time of war and rivalry, when a kingdom's future rested in the balance as a neighbor tried to extend its territory. It was also a time of artistic triumphs, when richly decorated stone temples were built to honor the gods. Indian kings met visitors from far away, and traders came for the region's spices.

SOUTHERN INDIA AND SRI LANKA

200s–1200s
Sri Lankan civilization flourishes.

300s–800s
Pallava kingdom period.

550s–1150s
Chalukya kingdom period.

700s–1300s
Pandya kingdom period.

800s–1200s
Chola kingdom period.

c. 1017
Cholas conquer Sri Lanka.

c. 1070
Cholas expelled from Sri Lanka.

1200s
Arab traders establish bases on Sri Lanka.

c. 1290
Marco Polo, a European traveler, visits southern India.

1411
Zheng He, a Chinese admiral, lands on Sri Lanka, captures the island's king and takes him back to China.

There are more than 100 ancient Hindu temples in Aihole, southern India, of which Durga temple is the most striking. Built about 700, it is dedicated to the Hindu god Vishnu. Little now remains of its tower.

The Chalukya Dynasty

Like other kingdoms of southern India, the Chalukyas were ruled by warrior kings, the first of whom was Pulakesi I (reigned 543–566). He made Aihole the first Chalukya capital. For 300 years, from the mid 500s, the Chalukyas fought rival kingdoms in an attempt to become the leading state in southern India. Their power in the region ended when their last king died in 1156.

Sri Lanka, the Spice Island

Sri Lanka—a large island off the south coast of India—has a long history of contact with its mainland neighbor. In the Medieval period the island changed hands between Sri Lankan and Indian rulers (Pandyas and Cholas). Buddhism was the principal religion, and the caste system divided people into social groups. Traders, particularly from Arabia, came to Sri Lanka for spices, which were highly prized.

A rockface at Mahabalipuram, port of the Pallavas, has a frieze of hundreds of figures.

Paintings on the wall of a Sri Lankan cave show the everyday fashions of women in the 600s.

Kingdom of the Pandyas

Based in the southern tip of India, the Pandyas were one of the region's oldest groups of people, whose ancestors had traded with ancient Egypt and Rome. As India divided into small kingdoms, the Pandyas came under the rule of the Pallavas and Cholas. But, in the 1250s, a powerful king helped them become the leading power in the south.

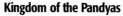

Kingdom of the Pallavas

The Pallava Kingdom dominated southeast India between the 300s and late 800s. Pallava merchants traded with Sri Lanka and Asia, and painting, literature and architecture flourished. At the port town of Mahabalipuram a magnificent temple to the Hindu god Shiva was built. When the Cholas began their rise to power in the 850s, the Pallava kings were unable to resist. Their kingdom fell to the Cholas and became part of their empire.

Pulakesi II (reigned 609–642), a Chalukya king, sits on a throne to receive envoys from Persia.

War elephants charge along the walls of Hoysaleswara temple at Halebidu, southern India.

Collapse of the Chola Empire

For 400 years, southern India and Sri Lanka were dominated by the Cholas until, in the 1200s, their empire began to fall apart. It came under pressure from Hoysala kings in the west, who took Chola territory and added it to their kingdom. Further strain came from the Pandyas in the south, who succeeded in conquering the remains of the Chola Empire in 1257. When the last Chola king, Rajendra IV, died in 1279, the Chola Dynasty ended.

A copper coin, thought to have been made and used by the Pandyas.

Mahmud of Ghazni listens as a storyteller recites a poem to him.

Muslim Rule in India

Mahmud of Ghazni

Between 1000 and 1030, Mahmud of Ghazni (a city and kingdom in Afghanistan and northeast Iran) invaded northern India on at least 17 occasions. Mahmud (971–1030) was a warlord and a devout Muslim, and his raids were especially harsh to the Hindus of India. He destroyed and looted Hindu temples and cities, and took their riches back to his capital at Ghazni, which he hoped would become as wealthy as Baghdad, Islam's leading city. Mahmud's vast armies of foot soldiers and cavalry conquered the Indian regions of Kashmir and Punjab, which he ruled through force. He did not, however, convert the Hindu population to Islam, although some Hindus served in his Muslim army.

Muslims had lived side by side with India's Hindus, Buddhists and Jains for centuries. They were trading partners who tolerated each other's different beliefs and cultures. However, when Muslims in neighboring Afghanistan began to take an interest in India's wealth, it led to a long period of conflict and the creation of an Islamic kingdom in northern India, known as the Sultanate of Delhi. The arrival of Islam had a great influence on Indian culture. It gave rise to a new language, and new styles of literature and architecture.

Traders and Conquerors

Muslims had traded with India for hundreds of years. Merchants visited west coast towns for cotton textiles and spices, but in the 1000s the subcontinent was invaded by Muslim armies from the northwest, beginning with the raids of Mahmud of Ghazni. There were further invasions by Turkish and Afghan Muslims in the 1100s, who made the city of Delhi the capital of their kingdom in northern India. Muslim control of the region peaked in the 1350s, and ended in the early 1500s.

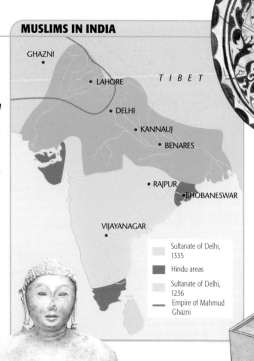

MUSLIMS IN INDIA

- GHAZNI
- LAHORE
- TIBET
- DELHI
- KANNAUJ
- BENARES
- RAJPUR
- BHOBANESWAR
- VIJAYANAGAR

Sultanate of Delhi, 1335
Hindu areas
Sultanate of Delhi, 1236
Empire of Mahmud Ghazni

The superb horsemanship of the Muslim invaders is celebrated on this pottery dish of the period.

Marble sculpture of a Jain "ford-maker" who shows followers the way to spiritual understanding.

The Jains

The Indian religion of Jainism was old by the time Islam came to the country. Followers, known as Jains, traced their religion back to the 500s BCE. They were vegetarians who lived as ascetics, leading simple lives that avoided worldly pleasures. As Islam spread, it met Jainism and the religions influenced each other. They shared ideas in art and architecture.

Great Mosque of Delhi

India's Muslim rulers made a lasting impression on the country's architecture. In Delhi, capital of Muslim India, they built the Quwat al-Islam mosque. Started in 1195, Indian stonemasons worked for 40 years to complete the massive building. At its center stood a minaret tower, built to commemorate the Muslim conquest of northern India.

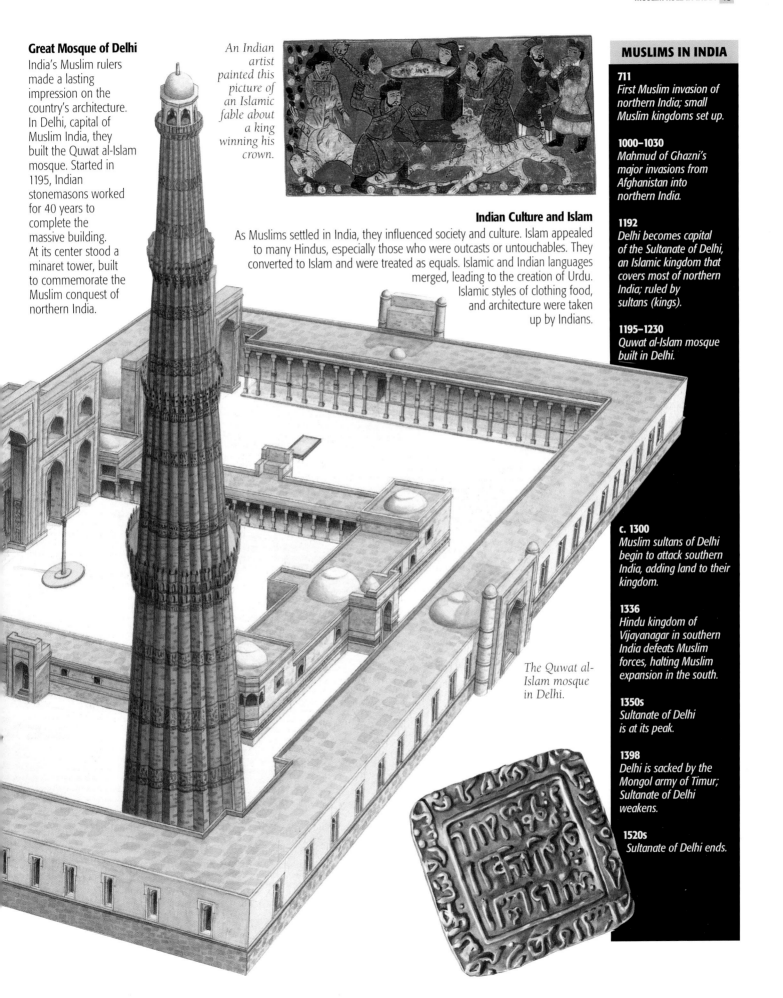

An Indian artist painted this picture of an Islamic fable about a king winning his crown.

Indian Culture and Islam

As Muslims settled in India, they influenced society and culture. Islam appealed to many Hindus, especially those who were outcasts or untouchables. They converted to Islam and were treated as equals. Islamic and Indian languages merged, leading to the creation of Urdu. Islamic styles of clothing food, and architecture were taken up by Indians.

The Quwat al-Islam mosque in Delhi.

MUSLIMS IN INDIA

711
First Muslim invasion of northern India; small Muslim kingdoms set up.

1000–1030
Mahmud of Ghazni's major invasions from Afghanistan into northern India.

1192
Delhi becomes capital of the Sultanate of Delhi, an Islamic kingdom that covers most of northern India; ruled by sultans (kings).

1195–1230
Quwat al-Islam mosque built in Delhi.

c. 1300
Muslim sultans of Delhi begin to attack southern India, adding land to their kingdom.

1336
Hindu kingdom of Vijayanagar in southern India defeats Muslim forces, halting Muslim expansion in the south.

1350s
Sultanate of Delhi is at its peak.

1398
Delhi is sacked by the Mongol army of Timur; Sultanate of Delhi weakens.

1520s
Sultanate of Delhi ends.

Glossary

Ascetics People who live very simply and deny themselves worldly comforts and pleasures, usually for religious reasons.

Basin A low-lying, roughly bowl-shaped area of land which is drained by a river and its streams.

Buddhism A religion based on the teachings of Buddha (c. 566–480 BCE). Buddhists believe that human beings face endless reincarnations (rebirths and deaths) unless they gain release through wisdom and peace.

Bushido The Japanese samurai's code of honor, which was influenced by Buddhism. The main rule was to be willing to die at any moment in the service of one's lord.

Castes The hereditary classes that make up the varna social divisions of Hindu society in India. Members of a caste can marry only people within the same caste, and they each have traditional occupations that come to them as a birthright of their caste. There are thousands and thousands of castes in India today.

Calligraphy The art of beautiful handwriting, much admired in Medieval China and Japan.

Caravan A company of traders travelling together, usually with a train of camels, through the desert or along the Silk Road. The caravan was the safest means of transporting goods across Asia or the Sahara Desert.

Ceramic A hard, breakable material made by firing clay in an oven. Some of the finest works of art of Medieval Southeast Asia and China were works of ceramics, such as plates or vases.

City-states Independent cities that govern themselves through a council or a ruling family.

Clan A group of people belonging to the same tribe who are related or share a common mythical ancestor. Clans are often thought to have an animal founder and there are many examples of bear clans, eagle clans and the like.

Coptic An Afro-Asiatic language, written in the Greek alphabet. Also, anything that relates to the Coptic Church, an ancient Christian Church in Egypt.

Confucianism The philosophy of the Chinese thinker Confucius (551–479 BCE), which emphasizes education, respect for ancestors, and a well-ordered society.

Dakinis In the Buddhist religion, supernatural beings that have been compared with elves or angels and which help to develop the believer's spirituality.

Daimyo Any of a group of powerful landowners that dominated much of Japan from the 11th to the 19th centuries.

Dynasty A line of rulers coming from the same family, or a period during which they reign.

Ebony The hard, dark wood found in tropical trees, much prized for its use in delicate carvings and furniture.

Envoy A messenger sent by a government on a special mission and who acts as a representative of the government or state.

Exile The condition of having been forced to leave one's homeland.

Guild A group of people belonging to the same trade or profession, who band together to protect their common interests.

Hinduism The main religion of India, which involves the worship of many gods, a belief in reincarnation (being born again in another life) and a caste system.

Iron Age The period in human development following the Bronze Age in which people used iron to make weapons and tools. One of the Metal Ages.

Ivory The teeth of certain mammals. Elephant ivory is the most abundant form, which are the long, external upper incisors of the animal, commonly called tusks. Ivory is a very dense, usually whitish material that is easily carved and worked.

Jainism An ancient form of the Hindu religion, with its own scriptures.

Monolith A statue, an obelisk or a column carved from a huge block of stone.

Mosque A Muslim place of worship.

Mother-of-pearl The hard, shiny substance found inside the shells of certain mollusks, such as the oyster. Mother-of-pearl can be carved into fine objects or inlaid into furniture.

Muslims Followers of the religion of Islam who worship one God and honor the Prophet Muhammad, who wrote the Qur'an.

Nomadic Term used to describe a member of a tribe who travels from place to place in search of grass for animals. A person who wanders and does not settle down in any particular place.

Plateau An elevated, relatively flat, stretch of land.

Procession The act of a group of people marching in a formal way for a religious ceremony, a ritual parade.

Shinto The name of the native religion of Japan. Believers worship a number of gods, from whom the emperor is thought to be descended.

Shogun A Japanese hereditary military dictator who had greater power than the emperor.

Smelting The process of melting ores, mineral deposits containing a metal, to separate the metal from the rock.

Sultan A royal ruler of a Muslim country.

Taoism A popular Chinese philosophy that argues for a simple, honest life and the noninterference in the course of natural events.

Terra-cotta Hard, unglazed earthenware, made from clay. Early cultures made pottery and sculpture from terra-cotta.

Typhoon A violent tropical storm, especially in the China seas. The word comes from the Chinese words *tai*, meaning "great," and *fung*, meaning "wind."

Yurt A circular tent made with a framework of poles and covered in felt and animal skins. The yurt was used by the Mongols in Central Asia. It could be taken down easily and packed onto animals.

Index

Abbasid caliphs 14
Abouji (Liao Dynasty founder) 22
Adulis 9
Afghanistan 44, 45
Africa 4, 5, 6, 7, 8, 9, 10, 11, 12, 13, 14, 15
Aguda, Jurchen clansman 22
Aihole 39, 42
–Durga Temple 42
Akan region 11, 12
Al-Biruni (Arab scholar) 39
Alexandria 9, 10, 14
Almoravid emirate 10
Alwa, Kingdom of 10, 15
Anbuk 33
Angkor 5, 34, 35
Anuradhapura 39, 40
Arabia 12, 13, 14, 15, 40, 42
Arabian Sea 40
Arabs 16, 42
Asia 5, 6, 7, 13, 16, 22, 16
Atlantic Ocean 9, 10, 13
Axum 4, 8, 9, 10, 13, 14

Bactria, 16
Baghdad 14, 44
Bantu 9
Bantu-speakers 6, 9
Bay of Bengal 39, 40
Beijing *see* Dadu *and* Yenjing
Benares 39, 44
Benin 5, 10, 11
Benue River 8, 9
Berber kingdoms 8
Berbers 14, 15
Bhobaneswar 44
Bi, Sheng (inventor of printing) 19
Bigo 10
Bing, Di, Song emperor 19
Bini (Edo) people 11
Black Death 24
Bohai 16
Borneo 16, 34, 36
Borobudur 34, 37
   –Temple of 37
Broederstroom 9
Buddha, the 29, 37
Buddhism 4, 7
–in China 16, 19 20, 24, 36
–in India 38, 39, 40, 41, 44
–in Japan 26, 27, 29
–in Korea 32, 33
–in Southeast Asia 34, 35, 36, 37
–Tantric 41
Burmese Kingdom *see* Myanmar
Byzantine Empire 6, 14

Caesarea 9

Cairo 10, 13
Cambodia 4, 5, 34, 35, 36 *see also* Khmer Empire
Cameroon 8
Carthage 8
caste system 39, 42
Ceylon 16
Ch'a Ching ("Tea Classics") 16
Chabi (Wife of Kublai Khan) 25
Chad, Lake 4, 10
Champa 16
Chang'an 6, 16, 20, 21, 23, 26
Chang Jiang (Yangtze River) 21
Chauan 38
China 4, 5, 6, 7, 13, 16, 17, 18, 19, 20, 21, 22, 23, 24, 25, 26, 30, 32, 33, 36, 42
–Five Dynasties and Ten Kingdoms period 5, 18, 19
–Song dynasty 5, 6, 18, 19, 22, 23, 24, 25
–Tang dynasty 4, 6, 16, 17, 18, 20, 21
–Yuan dynasty 5, 24
Chingis Khan (Temujin) 22, 23, 24, 25
Christianity 8, 14, 15
Confucianism 24
Congo 15
Congo Basin 10
Congo River 8, 9
Constantinople 6
Coptic Church 7, 14
Ctesiphon 6

Dadu (Beijing) 23, 24
dakinis 41
Damascus 6, 14
Dan no Ura, Battle of 28
daimyo 30
Deccan Plateau 38, 39
Delhi 5, 39, 44, 45
–Quwat al-Islam mosque 45
Deogiri 39
Diamond Sutra 16
Djenné 14, 15
Do Dimmi 9

East Africa 9, 11, 13
East Asia 20, 26
East China Sea 16
Edo (Bini) people 11
Egypt, 6, 7, 14, 42
Ethiopia 9, 14, 15
Europe 16, 23
Ezana, Axumite king 8

Gambia 10
Ganesha, Hindu god 36

Gangaikondacholapuram 40
–Gangaikonda Temple 41
Ganges River 39, 40, 41
Gao 10
Gaozu (Li, Yuan), Tang emperor 16, 20
Gempei War, the 30
Ghana, Kingdom of 4, 10, 11
Ghazni 44
Guangzhou port 21
Guinea 10
Gujarat 38
Gwalior 39

Halebidu 43
–Hoysaleswara Temple 43
Han, Huang (Chang'an artist) 20
Hariharala 34
Harsha Vardana 38, 39
Hazni 39
Heiankyo (Kyoto) 4, 21, 26, 28, 30
Heiji, Battle of 28
Heijokyo (Nara) 4, 21, 26, 27, 28
–Horyu-ji Temple 27
Hephthalites, Empire of the 6
Herat 23
Hinduism 34, 36, 41, 44, 45
Honshu Island 26, 27, 30
Hoysala kings 43
Huang He River (Yellow River) 6, 21, 24
Hue 33
Huangzhou 19
Huizong, Song emperor 19
Huns 38

Ife, Kingdom of 5, 10
India 4, 5, 6, 12, 13, 16, 34, 42, 43
–Chandella Kingdom 5, 39
–Chalukya Dynasty 39, 40, 42
–Chola Empire 4, 5, 40, 41, 42, 43
–Delhi, Sultanate of 5, 44, 45
–Gupta Empire 6, 38, 39
–Harsha Empire 4, 38, 39
–Pallavas, Kingdom of the 5, 41, 42, 43
–Pandyas, Kingdom of the 5, 41, 42, 43
–Pratihara Empire 39
–Vijayanaga, Kingdom of 5, 44, 45

Indian Ocean 6, 12, 13, 34, 40
Indonesia 36, 37, 40
Iran 44
Iron Age 8
Irrawaddy River 35
Isanapura 34
Islam 7, 10, 14, 15, 36, 44, 45

Jainism 44
Japan 4, 5, 6, 7, 16, 20, 15, 30, 31, 33
–Asuka period 4, 26, 27
–Heian period 5, 28, 29
–Kamakura period 5, 30
–Kofun period 6
–Nara period 26, 27, 28
Japanese clans
–Genji 28
–Fujiwara 28
–Heike 28, 30, 31
–Minamoto 30, 31
–Soga 26, 27
Java 34, 36, 37
Jayavarman II, Khmer king 35
Jenne-jeno 4, 6, 8, 9, 10, 15
Jianzhen (Chinese monk) 20
Jin Empire 5, 19, 22
Jurchen tribes 22

Kabul 23
Kaegyong 33
Kaifeng 5, 18, 19, 22, 23
Kamakura 30
Kammu, Japanese emperor 28
Kanchi 40
Kanchipuram 39
Kanem, Kingdom of 4, 10
Kannauj 39, 44
Karakorum 23
Kashmir 16
Kashmir 44
Katuruta 9
Keita, Sundiata 14
Kenya 12
Khajuraho 38, 39
Khitan tribes 22
Khmer Empire, the 4, 5, 16, 34, 35
Khoisan-speakers 9
Khubilai Khan 5, 24, 25
Kilwa 12, 13
Kolkoi 39
Korea 4, 5, 6, 7, 20, 21, 26
–Goguryeo, Kingdom of 32
–Koryo (Goryeo), Kingdom of 5, 32, 33
–Paekche, Kingdom of 4, 32
–Parhae, Kingdom of 32, 33
–Period of the Three Kingdoms 32
–Silla, Kingdom of 4, 16, 21, 32, 33
Kufah 6
Kufic script 6
Kumbi Saleh 13
Kyongju 21, 33
Kyushu Island, 28, 30

Lahore 44

Lakeswar, Buddhist god 39
Lalibela (Roha) 10, 14, 15
Lalibela, Ethiopian k7ing 15
Lan Chang 34
Laos 35, 36
Liao dynasty 22
Liao valley 22
Liaoyang 23, 33
Longmen caves 17
Luoyang 16

Madura 39, 40
Magadha, Kingdom of 38
Mahabalipuram 42, 43
Mahmoud of Ghazni 44, 45
Maitreya, Buddha of the Future 17
Makkura, Kingdom of 10
Malaysia 34
Maldive Islands 40
Mali 5, 9, 10, 11, 12, 13, 14
Malindi 12, 13
Manchuria 5, 19, 22
Mark, Apostle 14
Marrakech 14, 15
–Kutubiya mosque 15
Mauritania 9, 11
Mecca 10
Mediterranean Sea 12, 13
Meroë 8, 9
Minamoto Yoritomo 30, 31
Mogadishu 12, 13
Mon people 35
Mongols 5, 19, 22, 23, 24, 25, 30,
    32, 33, 34, 35
Morocco 14
Mouila 9
Muhammad the Prophet 6, 7, 14
Munmu, Wang, King of Silla 4, 32,
    33
Murasaki, Shikibu (author) 28, 29
–The Tale of Genji 28, 29
Musa, Mansa 10
Muslims 5, 7, 11, 14, 15, 24, 36, 38-
    in India 44, 45
Myanmar (Burma) 34, 35, 40

Ndora 9
Neo-Confucianism 19
Niger River 6, 8, 9, 11
Nigeria 8, 9, 10, 11
Nok culture 4, 6, 8, 9
North Africa 6, 8, 15
Nubia 6, 7, 8, 14
Numidia 9

Ogodei Khan 22
Otrar 23
Oyo, Kingdom of 10

Pacific Ocean 28, 30

Pagan 34, 35
Panduranga 34
Pemba Island 12, 13
Periplus of the Erytharaean, The 13
Persia 6, 16, 43
Philippines 16
Polo, Marco 24, 42
Polonnaruwa 39
Portuguese 11
Prithviraj III, Rajput king 38, 39
Pulakesi I, Chalukya king 42
Pulakesi II, Chalukya king 43
Punjab 44
Puyu 33
Pyongyang 33
Pyu people 35

Qu'ran, the 15

Rajaraja I, Chola king 40
Rajastan 39
Rajendra I, Chola king 40, 41
Rajendra IV, Chola king 41, 43
Rajpur 44
Rajputana 38, 39
Red Sea 9, 13
Rig Veda 39
Roha (Lalibela) 10, 14, 15
Roman Empire 6
Romans, ancient 6, 8
Rome 6, 42
Ruanruan, Empire of the 6
Russian principalities 23

Sahara Desert 8, 9, 10, 12, 13, 15
Samarkand 24, 25
Samurai 30, 31
Sassanid Empire 6
Scythians 38
Sea of Japan 28, 30
Senegal 10, 11
Seoul 33
Shikoku Island 28, 30
Shinto religion 29
Shiva, Hindu god 41, 43
shoguns 5, 30, 31
Shona Empire 10, 12
Shotoku, Prince 26, 27
Silk Road 6, 7, 16, 21
Somalia 12
Songhai Empire 10
South China Sea 34
Southeast Asia 4, 5, 7, 16, 34, 35, 36
Southern Africa 8, 9, 10, 12
Sri Lanka 40, 41, 42, 43
Su, Shi (Su Tungpo, Chinese
    calligrapher) 19
Sudan 7, 8, 9, 14
Sui emperors 6, 16

Sukhotai 34
Sumatra 34, 36, 40
Swahili 12, 13

Taika reforms 26
Taiyuan 16
Taizong, Song emperor 16, 18, 20
Taizu (Zhao Kuangyin), Song
    emperor 18, 19
Takrur, Kingdom of 10
Tamerlane see Timur
Tangier 10
Tanjore 40, 41
Tanzania 12
Taoism 19, 24
Taoudenni 13
Taruga 9
Temujin see Genghis Khan
Thailand 5, 34, 36
–Chiang Mai kingdom 5, 34
Thang Long (Hanoi) 34
Thaton 34
Tibet 16, 20, 39, 44
Timbuktu 10, 13, 14
Timur (Tamerlane), Mongol leader
    24, 25, 45
Tingis 9
Toghon Temur, Yuan emperor 24
Tokyo 30
Tunis 10
Turkestan 20
Turkish invaders 39
Turkish nomads 20
Turks, Ottoman 25

Udaipur (Mewar) 39
Umayyad dynasty 6, 14
Urdu (language) 45
Urgench 23
Uzbekistan 25

Vandals 6
Vatapi 39
Vietnam 4, 5, 20, 34, 36
–Cham Kingdom 4, 5, 34, 35
Vijaya 34
Vijayalaya, Chola king 40, 41
Vishnu, Hindu god 42
Visigoths 6

Wagadu see Ghana, Kingdom of
West Africa 6, 9, 13
Wu, Zetian, Tang empress 17, 20

Xuanzang (Chinese pilgrim) 16, 39
Xuanzong, Tang emperor 16

Yangang caves 7
Yangtze River (Chang Jiang) 21
Yellow Sea 33

Yenjing (Beijing) 22
yurts 22, 23
Yoruba 5, 10
Yusuf, Almoravid leader 14

Zagwe dynasty 15
Zanzibar 15
–Kizimakazi Mosque 15
Zao Gonen 28
Zhao, Mengfu (Chinese artist) 24,
    25
Zhaoxuan, Tang emperor 16
Zheng, He (Chinese admiral) 42
Zhu, Xi (Confucian scholar) 19
Zhu, Yuanzhang, Ming emperor 24
Zimbabwe, Great 5, 9, 10, 12, 13